Engaging Millennials
for Ethical Leadership

Engaging Millennials for Ethical Leadership

What Works for Young Professionals and Their Managers

Jessica McManus Warnell

BUSINESS EXPERT PRESS

Engaging Millennials for Ethical Leadership:
What Works for Young Professionals and Their Managers

First published in 2015 by
Business Expert Press, LLC
222 East 46th Street, New York, NY 10017
www.businessexpertpress.com

ISBN-13: 978-1-60649-988-7 (paperback)
ISBN-13: 978-1-60649-989-4 (e-book)

Business Expert Press Giving Voice to Values on Business Ethics
and Corporate Social Responsibility Collection

Collection ISSN: 2333-8806 (print)
Collection ISSN: 2333-8814 (electronic)

Cover and interior design by S4Carlisle Publishing Services
Private Ltd., Chennai, India

First edition: 2015

10 9 8 7 6 5 4 3 2 1

Printed in the United States of America.

Dedication

To the first author I ever knew, Linda DeCicco,
and my fearless father, Don McManus.

Abstract

By 2020, half of America's workforce will be millennials; by 2050, millennials will represent 75 percent of the global workforce. Corporate trainings and consultant workshops-for-hire on dealing with this influx abound, but how, specifically and with impact, can young professionals and their companies flourish? In this era of transparency and accountability, explorations of effective organizations are inseparable from considerations of ethical leadership. How can we best prepare the millennials for productive and positive careers? Can managers leverage the unique skills and talents of this generation toward shared goals and business success? Designed for millennials and their managers, we consider how we can cultivate the strengths of this generation toward a new business paradigm. *Engaging Millennials for Ethical Leadership* provides strategies for optimizing performance at work, drawing on emerging research and complemented with perspectives gleaned from students at a top-tier business school and from a diverse group of corporate executives. The book is structured around millennial capacities and inclinations, with each chapter dedicated to specific characteristics and including manager action items for each. We explore the *Giving Voice to Values* framework as one promising approach to managing millennials, with its focus on enhancing our capacities for ethical action. Through strategic attention to hiring, training, and development, organizations can capitalize on the promise of these new professionals. Companies are compelled to consider these issues for two primary reasons: (1) to attract, develop, and retain top talent, these characteristics, dynamics, and processes must be explored; (2) we are in the midst of a new business paradigm, and many of the gifts and proclivities of this generation of emerging leaders can be leveraged to strengthen and grow effective, ethical organizations that will flourish in this context.

Keywords

Managing millennials, *Giving Voice to Values,* millennials at work, millennials and ethics, ethical cultures at work

Table of Contents

Acknowledgments

This book was written with the generous support of the Notre Dame Deloitte Center for Ethical Leadership. Ed Conlon, the faculty director of the Center, builds bridges every day between the academic and practitioner community that are critical contributions to the progression from knowledge to action. Adam Kronk, the center program director, co-presenter on iterations of this work, early reviewer, idea-exchanger and all-around wonderful colleague, contributed greatly to the project.

Thank you to the team at Business Expert Press for their guidance and support.

The foundation of this work is the *Giving Voice to Values* approach to professional development. Its creator and director, Mary C. Gentile, is unfailingly supportive, selfless in her commitment to improving business and business education, and dedicated to true realization of the potential of business for good. I am grateful to and inspired by her.

Thank you to Carolyn Woo for introducing Mary Gentile and the *Giving Voice to Values* approach to the Mendoza College of Business, and for her model, mentorship, and support. Thanks to our department chair, David Hartvigsen, and our dean, Roger Huang, for their leadership in developing students and faculty who strive to "Ask More of Business."

My colleagues at Notre Dame, especially Professors Robert Audi, Georges Enderle, Joseph Holt, Brian Levey, Patrick E. Murphy, William Nichols, Ann Tenbrunsel, and Oliver Williams, have consistently shared expertise and support; I am grateful for our learning community. Additional thanks to Pat Murphy for allowing me to incorporate his helpful tool, the *Ethical Recruiting Guide*, into this book.

Thank you to my friends and colleagues at Reitaku University in Kashiwa-shi, Chiba-ken, Japan, particularly Professors Toru Umeda and Kaori Takamoto, whose expertise and enthusiasm have expanded my sensibilities about achieving our best selves.

My student research assistants Kirsten Conrath, Marco Ruiz, Lauren Barnes, and Kalley McMullen provided tremendous help—I am excited to see how these brilliant young millennials make their mark in the world.

Thank you to Della Dewald for her photography and to the entire Dewald family for their example of stellar human beings.

Thanks to Christopher Adkins at William & Mary for his invaluable feedback on early drafts of this work. His expert contributions to *Giving Voice to Values* and promoting excellence in business and social responsibility are an inspiration.

The corporate leaders who participated in our survey research and interviews are at the front lines of business responsibility every day. Their commitment to nurturing new leaders and realizing the potential of business for good critically informed this exploration; their expertise and contributions are appreciated greatly. Special thanks to Juliann Jankowski, Sharon Keane and Angeline Johnson, Jean Collier, Regina Emberton, Michael DeCicco, Angela Sekerka, Karl Sekerka, and others who shared the survey with their professional networks.

I am so grateful for the opportunity to work every day with such bright, passionate, and thoughtful students at Notre Dame. This Gen-Xer is energized, challenged, and inspired by these millennials every day, and I thank them, particularly those students in the *Managing and Milllennials* and *Giving Voice to Values* classes—watching you make your way in the world and contribute in so many ways is a privilege.

My family is my greatest joy, including my sisters Angela and Erin and their families, and especially my two sons (Generation Z?), Satchel and Benjamin. Thank you.

Introduction

"The Millennials Are Coming!"

"A new breed of American worker is about to attack everything you hold sacred: from giving orders, to your starched white shirt and tie. They are called, among other things, "millennials." There are about 80 million of them, born between 1980 and 1995, and they're rapidly taking over from the baby boomers who are now pushing 60. They were raised by doting parents who told them they are special, played in little leagues with no winners or losers, or all winners. They are laden with trophies just for participating, and they think your business-as-usual ethic is for the birds. And if you don't like it, you can take your job and shove it."[1]

Morley Safer, *60 Minutes*, CBS

Energy and passion around the topic of millennials in the workforce is palpable. By 2020, half of America's workforce will be millennials;

by 2050, millennials will represent 75 percent of the global workforce. Corporate trainings and consultant workshops-for-hire on dealing with this influx abound, but how, specifically and with impact, can young professionals and their companies flourish? Several helpful resources provide tips and strategies for general management of this new talent; I recommend some later in this volume. My focus here is the intersection between ethics and values, and effectively engaging young professionals toward building sustainable, successful businesses. In this era of transparency and accountability, explorations of effective organizations are inseparable from considerations of ethical leadership. Can millennials and their managers incorporate the dual goals of effective and ethical business? How can we best prepare millennials—today's business students and emerging professionals—for productive and positive careers? Can managers leverage the unique skills and talents of this generation toward shared goals and business success?

I developed this book in response to a disconnect between what appears in the press, and what my colleagues and I see every day in classrooms and on campuses and what we learn from corporate partners at all levels of business. To judge by media coverage such as the *60 Minutes* piece, millennials do not have much to offer. They are fairly consistently portrayed as entitled, lazy narcissists. Yet, these stereotypes do not resonate with my own experiences, nor with what emerging research tells us.

For over 10 years, I have had the good fortune of teaching hundreds of undergraduate business students each semester at a top-ranked U.S. business school. Absolutely, our students and young alumni, and their counterparts all over the country, spend a lot of time on their smartphones, have grand expectations for work–life balance, and possess many of the other stereotypes about "kids these days". . . . Yet they also start b-corps and social ventures, develop financial literacy programs for the most vulnerable, create impact investing initiatives, solve intractable problems with efficiency and commitment, and contribute to, manage, and own innovative, ethical businesses with tremendous positive impact.

Three years ago, I developed a course called *Managing Millennials,* and from day one the course was an interactive, iterative opportunity for these undergraduate business students in their senior year of college to push back on these stereotypes—and recognize where they rang true—and acknowledge that both emerging professionals and those who manage them must take steps toward the table for effective engagement toward shared goals. Managers can be instrumental in fostering alignment between millennials' expressed values, interests, and objectives at work with those values, and the decisions that reflect them, in their companies.

Of course, effective professional impact can not be considered distinctly from considerations of ethical business. Explicit attention to ethics in the business school has been part of our program since its inception. Along the way I have been tremendously grateful for and inspired by the opportunity to utilize *Giving Voice to Values* (GVV)[2], an innovative approach to professional development in business, developed by a remarkable scholar, mentor, and friend, Mary C. Gentile, PhD. In addition to many courses devoted to ethics in the core business disciplines of accountancy, finance, management, and marketing, since 2008 my university has offered the first dedicated undergraduate business course in GVV. Students consider topics derived from organizational behavior, psychology, cognitive neuroscience, and applied ethics to explore actionable, values-based decision making in business. This book evolved from these experiences and, I hope, reflects the optimism and promise of emerging professionals who have chosen business as their path toward contribution and engagement.

So as popular media lament the failings of the millennial generation and management experts resignedly sigh and focus on making do, we consider what might happen if we change the frame, and leverage the strengths of the millennial generation toward a new business paradigm. *Engaging Millennials for Ethical Leadership* provides strategies for optimizing performance and ethical commitment in the corporate context, complemented with perspectives gleaned from students at a top-tier business school and from a diverse group of corporate executives.

The book, designed for millennials and their managers, is structured around millennial capacities and inclinations, with each chapter dedicated to specific characteristics. Chapter 1 provides an introduction to the context of today's business, explores why this generational cohort is so important to business, and provides an overview of millennial traits. We then present an introduction to the GVV approach as an effective strategy for engaging young talent toward values-driven organizational goals.

Next we explore the characteristics of these young people, and how they influence our business culture. My contention is that many of these characteristics can be leveraged toward building ethical organizations, and each chapter explores the connections between millennial traits and the potential for ethical impact. One of the most salient issues for millennials is fluency with technology. Chapter 2 explores this new reality, including social media, at work. Most of us work with colleagues from many generations. Chapter 3 examines some of the challenges and opportunities around collective engagement of multigenerational talent at work. In Chapter 4, we discuss millennials' penchant for, and the promise of, professional mentorship—both leader-led and peer-to-peer. Chapter 5 presents a discussion of values at work—and millennials' expressed desire to "do well" and "do good."

Lastly, to both inspire and illustrate, we hear from the frontlines of business. Chapter 6 provides the results of existing research and our own explorations of millennials' values, interests, and challenges in their own words, and Chapter 7 presents example best practices gleaned from corporate profiles and our own interviews with professionals from a variety of industries.

To complement our discussion, we conducted our own examination of millennials at work. We interviewed a group of 22 senior business students and surveyed 138 more business sophomores, juniors and seniors at a top U.S. business school, to learn from their perceptions and aspirations. We also include perspectives from 75 senior business students reflecting on their own specific recommendations for millennial management, developed after taking a course on the topic. Additionally, we surveyed 65 executives from diverse industries, ranging from small companies with one employee to large with over 200,000 employees, and with annual revenues of $40,000 to over $35 billion USD.[3] The student and corporate perspectives offer helpful insights to inform our exploration.

Thus, *Engaging Millennials for Ethical Leadership* explores these millennial characteristics, strengths, and challenges, drawing on emerging research and corporate best practices. These characteristics can absolutely be a net positive for organizations—they can be harnessed to create both more economically successful as well as more ethical organizations. The book will consider why effective, ethical leadership is critical in a global context where sustainability is an obligatory backdrop. Equipping young professionals to contribute in today's businesses requires explicit attention to acknowledging the variety of stakeholders impacted by business in society.

Building on the GVV approach, which we describe in Chapter 1, the book prompts readers toward practical application of values-based decisions in real-world contexts of professional life. The GVV tenets of acknowledging choice, aligning actions with values through self-assessments and explorations of purpose, and examining common reasons and rationalizations for not acting on values, can provide a foundational professional development approach for millennials and their managers. Equipping emerging leaders with relevant and practical fluency in values-based decision making requires teaching thoughtful analyses and actionable skills. Millennials are primed for a managerial approach that channels their strengths (and challenges) into action-oriented, values-based contribution and leadership.

Companies are compelled to consider these issues for two primary reasons: (1) to echo the warning sounded on *60 Minutes*, the millennials *are* coming—to attract, develop, and retain top talent, these characteristics, dynamics, and processes must be explored; (2) we are in the midst of a new business paradigm, and many of the gifts and proclivities of this generation of emerging leaders can be leveraged to strengthen and grow effective, ethical organizations that will flourish in this context. A caveat—while this book is written from the perspective of an American academic using American student and corporate examples, my hope is that many of these approaches will resonate in other global contexts. The GVV approach has been piloted in hundreds of academic and business settings on all seven continents and is growing all the time. Many of our challenges are global and interconnected. This book is intended to be a resource for exploring how characteristics of millennials can contribute to organizations that represent the promise of business—a vibrant, ethical, innovative sector that has unmatched potential for impact.

CHAPTER 1

Millennials at Work

All photographs used with permission,
Copyright © 2014 by Della Dewald

Why Business? A Prosocial Conception

Young professionals and those who manage them are working in a challenging and tremendously exciting environment. In the public sphere,
business is typically presented representing two extremes—first, the
province of crooks, pursuing personal gain at the expense of societal
well-being, and second, those who seek to answer to the woes of society,
through diverse efforts including mega-philanthropy and social enterprise. As the business-scandal-of-the-day ticks along the bottom of our
television screens and the economy lumbers out of the financial crisis,

the ranks of students studying management, finance, accountancy, and marketing swell.[4] In the last several years, in the United States, more undergraduate and graduate business degrees were awarded than any other type of undergraduate or masters-level degree. Nearly one in three international undergraduates studying in the United States majors in business, management, or marketing.[5] As increasing calls for business accountability are offered alongside exciting movements that illustrate the business community's remarkable potential for good, emerging professionals may be left shaking their heads. Are business schools producing nothing more than "jargon-spewing economic vandals"[6] or is business, the institution with the agility, scale, reach, resources, and innovation to solve the world's most pressing problems, part of society's salvation?

Perhaps not surprisingly, my perspective is that business is one of the most critical components of solutions required for today's societal challenges. These two extremes—scourge or salvation—do not adequately account for business's role in our society. Effective, ethical business is a primary means to economic progress. It is instrumental to personal and community wealth, necessary new products and services, development of peaceful societies with adequate access to resources, new technologies that can address critical health needs, and so many other contributions toward personal, community, and global well-being. Equipping students studying business with the tools to channel their efforts accordingly recognizes the vast space in between these two extremes—the space in which most of us operate. So how do we prepare young professionals—today's students and workforce, tomorrow's leaders—to contribute in a sector in which the stakes are so high?

As we consider the impact of business in society, we must acknowledge the formative role of our business schools. Is teaching "business ethics" the answer to societal ills? These days, it is a rare business school that does not include some explicit attention to ethics in the curriculum. Yet pedagogy and practice differ tremendously. Consistent with outcomes from other studies,[7] students who have completed a course with substantive ethics content at one top-tier business school show a solid grasp of the concepts and theoretical foundations of ethical decision making, but still display room for growth in translating "knowing" to "doing."[8] Resembling the progression from memorizing theoretical management approaches to developing the acumen to execute them in the real world, opportunities exist around developing skills necessary for translating *moral intention* (a principled, reasoned analysis of an ethical dilemma: "I know what *should be done!*") to *application and behavior* (ethical action: "I *did* it, successfully!") in the business context. Scholars offer models for ethical decision making—we provide one model later in this volume—and management techniques for problem solving. Yet schools often struggle to teach strategies for effectively acting on those decisions—the critical step. We fail if we teach students how to discern the "right" thing to do, but then leave them unequipped to put their decision into action.

The call for actionable skills in values-based decision making also comes from the business community. Corporate studies indicate the market's demand for emerging leaders to possess proficiency in application, integration, problem solving, and fluency in broadly defined sustainability solutions.[9] Legislation such as Sarbanes-Oxley and Dodd-Frank arises, attempting to fill the void between ethical intention and action, and companies scramble to create a culture of internal resolution in the face of increasing incentives for whistleblowing. Urgent societal challenges—sustainability and global climate change, and globalization of business in the context of political, economic and social inequity and instability, among others—prompt business toward a triple bottom line approach to management that pursues financial, social, and environmental goals in the changing, global context.

Research tells us that millennials studying business display a strong commitment to prosocial enterprise.[10] They intend and expect to work for organizations whose missions align with their values of social engagement, sustainability, and other ethical considerations. At the same time, we know that managers often express struggles with engaging these emerging professionals in a way that channels this interest into productive organizational development. Today's global business demands actionable skills for ethical decision making and leadership. A common refrain from recruiters and managers of these young people is the gap between a firm grasp of theoretical business principles, and the skills to move toward action and implementation.

Educating and managing millennials in a way that bridges the gap between intention and action is critical. This challenge of translating the skills and content of "learning" to "doing" is a feat that all new professionals must master. In this era of nonstop information flow and global connectedness, the challenge of navigating and applying this information toward effective business is even more acute. Student proclivity, the need, and the demand for these skills are there. Millennials often can and do act on their values, and businesses can implement mechanisms to foster values-based decision making toward organizational culture and shared goals. As we consider strategies for equipping young professionals to operate successfully in this context, a promising approach is a framework called *Giving Voice to Values* (GVV). The GVV approach provides explicit and actionable professional development toward these goals and we will explore its key concepts and action items for millennials and their managers. We can recognize that the ways that millennial traits are experienced and expressed are critical, and through strategic attention to hiring, training, and development, organizations can capitalize on the promise of these new professionals.

So we begin in the spirit of optimism. When the topic of millennials at work arises at academic and professional conferences, and, as we will explore, in interviews with corporate leaders, it is inevitable that participants have horror stories of social media mavens gone rogue, demanding or unreliable new hires, and other grievances. These issues are real and they matter. Such frustration can easily dominate the dialogue and become immobilizing. In contrast, channeling the energies and talents of young professionals can help us create stronger, more vibrant, forward-looking organizations. Both sides have a role, with young people respecting organizational requirements—show up, work hard, learn from others, be committed—and managers fostering a culture of engagement and shared goals, incorporating the values of sustainability, values-based work, and balance. Our business schools can help prepare these young professionals. Our corporations can recognize, incentivize, and foster their gifts, talents, and passions. Both can prosper.

Who Are the Millennials?

Generally defined as young people who have graduated high school since the year 2000, or those born after 1980 but before 1995, these young professionals will soon represent a majority of the global workforce. As with most attempts to standardize large groups, scholars disagree on the boundaries, with the empirical data suggesting often contradictory characteristics of this cohort. Readers of this book, millennials or otherwise, may see themselves and this cohort in these pages, or not at all. The variance in empirical results reflects a gift of this generation—this may be the most diverse group of emerging businesspeople ever seen. Our exploration is about generalities, and is undertaken in the spirit of maximizing professional and organizational effectiveness. Young professionals are working in an environment in which these generalities are widely perceived, so by exploring them, we can enhance our capacities together. Thus, despite some differences in the values and virtues ascribed to this generation, a general consensus emerges around several key characteristics that can drive our strategies for effective engagement. These characteristics include the following:

- technological fluency and facility with social media;
- proclivity to multitask;
- teamwork capacities;
- a preference for training and mentorship to reflect sustained and personal attention;
- a desire for meaningful and fulfilling work;
- an increasing awareness of social and environmental sustainability issues.[11]

In addition, *immediacy* might be a helpful term to frame our thinking around this cohort. Identified as a core value of the millennials,[12] a desire for rapid response to queries, reaction to achievement, connection with others, and other manifestations of an open, quick, and continuous feedback loop characterize millennials more than any generation before. This desire, of course, can pose challenges for managers. As we will explore in Chapter 2, it can be channeled more positively toward ethical, effective organizations.

The reality is that most of us operate in multigenerational workplaces. Much is made (including in this volume!) about differences by generational cohort. But the nature of the challenge prompts critical considerations for professional and organizational development. A research finding with helpful implications can be considered here. Thus, although broad differences can be observed between generational groups at work, interestingly, specific characteristics seem to differ by institution.[13] These generational traits and characteristics manifest themselves in different ways depending on the organizational culture and conditions. This finding suggests that *how these differences are experienced and expressed matters*, and that *the ways these traits are managed makes a difference.* Managers have tremendous potential for impacting the ways millennials engage with their work, and are encouraged to interpret these generalizations as they apply to their specific companies.

Thus, the ways these intergenerational differences are acknowledged and translated into employment skills can be enhanced strategically by the organization through the approach to hiring, training, and developing its talent. GVV is an approach that provides tangible strategies to enhance engagement of millennials and to effectively manage multigenerational cultures.

Why Now?

The question may be raised—is the "back in my day" plaintive view of the next generation simply cyclical? Does not every generation lament the one that follows? While certainly this dynamic is not exclusive to the ascension of the millennials, several features of this generation and the era in which they are coming of age merit our close attention and demand response from business leaders. First, millennials, as children of the baby boomers, numerically represent a proportion of the business community—employees, managers, and consumers—that will be unmatched. There are nearly *90 million* people in this age group in the United States alone. This bodes well for the American economy—the youngest of these young people (there are more 23-year-olds than any other age group in the United States[14]) are the most aggressive about avoiding and paying down consumer debt, are starting their careers largely missing the worst of the economic recession, and through sheer size will help create and sustain employment and wealth.[15] The ranks of millennials in management are increasing tremendously. As noted above, business degrees are being awarded now more than ever—in the United States, more than any other type of degree.

Yet other issues are perhaps even more important. Critically, technology is a multiplier. These generational characteristics are more acute and impactful because their reach and scope are much broader. Relatedly, we are in an era of transparency never before experienced. Corporate responsibility (and lack thereof) is regularly tweeted around the world in less time than it takes us to complete this sentence. In some cases, we know, minutiae by minutiae, what one another are doing like never before. Privacy challenges abound. This transparency and constant communication influences who we are and what we do. It changes the playing field for employee recruitment and retention, as job seekers (and, of course, consumers, investors, competitors, and other stakeholders) have instant access to information on policies and procedures of companies—those they desire, and those they seek to avoid. Accountability has changed—pro- and antisocial behavior is visible and we, as individuals, and as corporations, are increasingly subject to influence and to be influenced.

Because of these advances, business is operating in a global context where geographic borders no longer limit us—they are permeable and regularly penetrated. We source products and labor around the world. Our shared context leads to shared concerns. The stakes are higher. We ignore the changing nature of business, and the interconnectedness of business leadership and ethical considerations, at our peril—and at the risk of jeopardizing our people and our planet. The GVV approach is a resource for navigating these challenges.

The *Giving Voice to Values* Framework

GVV is a new framework for values-driven professional development that draws on organizational behavior, social psychology, cognitive neuroscience, and management research, in addition to observation and interaction with top business schools and corporations around the globe. *Engaging Millennials for Ethical Leadership* explores the particular applicability of key concepts of the approach as resources for corporations to cultivate opportunity around millennial professionals. Because of this generation's gifts, talents, and challenges, GVV is well matched to foster professional development and effective organizational cultures. GVV, used successfully in hundreds of business schools, companies, and other organizations around the world, and growing fast, has unique relevance to this cohort of young talent seeking to align values with work and contribute meaningfully to the corporations in which they are employed.

What is the GVV approach? We start with an assertion: regardless of our generational cohort, most of us would like to integrate who we are, and what we value, with what we do. Of course, research and experience demonstrate that values conflicts are inherent in professional life. The things we want to accomplish and the way we want to live often seem in conflict with expectations of clients, peers, bosses, and our organizations.[16] GVV was developed to help individuals acknowledge, clarify, speak, and act on their values in the face of these conflicts. It is a curriculum designed to maximize professional impact that has been used successfully with experienced professionals, emerging leaders, new hires, and graduate- and undergraduate-level students, and we will explore its alignment with and promise for engaging millennials toward organizational effectiveness.[a]

Importantly, considerations of ethical leadership and effective organizations are inseparable. One need only open a newspaper (or, in the spirit of our tech-savvy millennials, queue up the front page on a mobile device) to witness our ongoing challenges to effective, ethical business. Business schools and corporations at every level of employee engagement think carefully about cultivating ethical business leaders. Different approaches abound—from curricula and experiential opportunities to compliance trainings and character development—yet our best organizations universally recognize their role in developing the capacities of value-based

---

[a]This book presents several key components of the *Giving Voice to Values* approach to professional development. Much more material is available, including case studies, teaching notes, foundational readings and exercises, and self-assessment instruments. Faculty and professionals can adapt the GVV approach into stand-alone workshops, functional or topical modules within existing courses and activities, dedicated programs of studies, custom peer coaching programs or custom curriculum development and training exercises. Much of these materials are free for use, "open-source," with permission. See www.GivingVoicetoValues.org and www.GivingVoiceToValues TheBook.com for more information.

leaders. The GVV approach is particularly suited toward cultivating millennial talent and engaging young professionals toward ethical leadership.

GVV has been described as "post-decision making"—that is, once an individual determines what he or she would like to do, based on his or her values, how might an individual, in a given context, act on this decision? The power of the GVV approach is rooted in the idea that "if enough of us felt empowered—and were skillful and practiced enough—to voice and act on our values effectively on those occasions when our best selves are in the driver's seat, business would be a different place."[17] Our global, interconnected society demands this new paradigm for business. College students and emerging professionals in the workplace face societal and market demands for effective, implementable, ethical decision-making skills. Developing skills necessary for translating *intention* to *application and behavior* in the business context is a key goal of business education and a necessary aptitude of professional life. The progression from knowledge to action is critical.

This dynamic is echoed in corporate contexts. Common approaches to training around ethics and compliance certainly help, and we are encouraged by the proliferation of such programs in this era, yet they often do not go far enough. From compliance and ethics seminars to simulations and other technology-driven approaches, companies explicitly attend to decision making and behavioral expectations for ethical issues at work. Companies have developed some effective approaches and we explore these best practices further in Chapter 7. GVV is a unique contribution to personal and professional development. The *knowledge* is the content supplied by the company—its mission, values, and objectives—and the progression toward effectively *voicing and acting within this particular content* is the contribution of the GVV approach. The integration of *knowing* and *doing* is thus realized. We explore this much more in the chapters ahead.

The Pillars: *Giving Voice to Values*

Millennial characteristics reflect two broad categories—capacities and inclinations, or skills and tendencies, and preferences for integration of values (both personal and societal) into professional life. The seven "pillars" of the GVV approach are well aligned with these characteristics.[18] Throughout this volume we will explore the pillars and their promise for professional development of millennials and their managers. These pillars can provide a helpful framework for thinking about values at work, and embedded in each are ideas that can relate directly to enhancing millennials' potential for positive, ethical impact in their organizations. We begin with a brief introduction of each.

> The Pillars of *GVV*:
>> *Values*
>> *Choice*
>> *Normality*
>> *Purpose*
>> *Self-Knowledge and Alignment*
>> *Voice*
>> *Reasons and Rationalizations*

Values

When we discuss *values,* we are considering those values with an ethical dimension to them, a necessary deliberation as we explore successful personal and organizational development for millennials and their managers in today's professional environment. Often, questions of *which?* and *whose?* values can quickly dominate discussion of decision making—particularly in this increasingly globalized business environment. These considerations are important but ultimately can be disabling. A discussion of this challenge is beyond the scope of this exploration. There are broad frameworks companies can consider when identifying their mission and goals, and their organizational values in the global context. The United Nations Declaration of Human Rights, the UN Global Compact, ISO Standards and other attempts to universalize and operationalize values for organizational use provide helpful guidance.

Our pragmatic focus suggests we (1) identify and appeal to widely held values when facing ethical conflicts, and (2) allow that these universal values often motivate our desire for ethical action. These universal values—called hypernorms, moral obligations, or virtues—appear fairly consistently regardless of context. Rushworth Kidder's crosscultural studies[19] led him to identify consensus around the core values of honesty, respect, responsibility, fairness, and compassion. We include further discussion of these virtues in our decision model, presented in Appendix C. World religions, codes of conduct, cultural norms, and other guiding frameworks reflect these values broadly. Despite some differences, it is both useful and practical to consider our shared values as we move toward addressing aligning values with decision making at work. An exploration of millennial talent, a group of young professionals with expressed desire to integrate values with their work, is not complete without considering the ways we can leverage these desires toward successful, ethical businesses.

These shared values can provide common ground in our work. A useful position to adopt when we think about how to voice and act on values at work can be acknowledging that our disagreements and differences about values do not preclude that the development and pursuit of *shared goals*.[20] Again, in the spirit of practical implementation, our goal here is not to decide what to do—it is to determine how to do it. The approach is useful regardless of context if we acknowledge our shared values and the shared space of the commons in today's business and society.

Choice

A foundational tenet of the GVV approach is acknowledging *choice*—the reality that despite pressures, ultimately we all possess the ability to decide how to respond to challenges at work, particularly those with a values or ethical dimension. This positioning of efficacy at work resonates well with millennials and can be leveraged toward organizational goals. As we explore millennial characteristics, we see their desire for a sense of contribution, impact, connection, and meaning at work—perhaps more acutely than in previous generations, and likely due to their upbringing—and this desire can be channeled in ways that align with the goals of successful, ethical organizations.

The "Action Item" exercise at the conclusion of this chapter provides a specific opportunity to consider how we put values into action. It is both empowering and enlightening to recognize the fact that we are all capable of speaking and acting on our values—we have done so in some instances, and we have not in others—and this exercise, "A Tale of Two Stories," allows us to explore this element of choice.[21] Considering specific instances of acting in accordance with our values, and instances when we have not, prompts us to reflect on choice. We have all exercised it. To "voice" our values, we must first acknowledge that we can, and do, act on our values—every day, personally and professionally.

Further, recognizing choice prompts self-knowledge and situational analysis. Being mindful about this reality is a necessary first step. Voicing values, explicitly acknowledged and considered, can develop our "muscle," our default habit. It can become a part of how we define ourselves.

Normality

What role do ethical questions play in professional life? If we consider workplace values conflicts as dilemmas that strike us without warning, it is no wonder that our immediate reaction to them is immobilization. If we see a dilemma as something to "get through" so that we can return to business as usual, we are marginalizing the ethical dimensions of work. Millennials are ahead of the game in this respect. They conceptualize business as inherently values-laden. Their experiences in business school and their coming of age in the post-Enron, current-financial-crisis era familiarize them with the disastrous effects of a values vacuum. Through technology and globalization, they have unprecedented access to witnessing the impact of best practices and corporate malfeasance in a variety of contexts.

At minimum, millennials' orientation acknowledges a risk-management conception of corporate responsibility. At their best, they pursue careers with, design and manage nimble, financially and ethically successful companies that integrate a triple bottom-line approach—consideration of ethical, environmental, and financial performance. These concerns have been part of their development as emerging professionals. These sensibilities can be translated into professional processes and decision-making capacity. The critical GVV element of moving from the often immobilizing contemplation of "*What is the right thing to do?*" to the questions "*What if you were going to act on your values? What would you say and do?"* progresses the issue away from lofty considerations of "right and wrong" to the practical.[22] The "hands-on, can do" approach favored by millennials is thus activated.

Thus, approaching careers with the expectation that values conflicts will be faced, and anticipating some of the most common types of conflicts characterizing our industries and our functional areas allow us to manage them much more effectively. We acknowledge our efficacy, our choice, and we can anticipate or *normalize* the idea that we may have to take risks to align with our values—we thus expand our understanding of the true degree of freedom we have in our decision making. We then experience these conflicts as normal and survivable, and we can more effectively and easily communicate with those who put us in these challenging situations.[23]

The integration of values as "business as usual" extends to organizational mission and processes. Scholars cite data from the Cone Millennial Cause Study[24] that indicates that nearly 80 percent of millennials explicitly desire to work for a company that is concerned with its contribution to society, and that millennials have internalized the need for societal contribution to include activities like volunteering for social causes. Further, millennials expect that the philanthropic approach to corporate social responsibility (CSR) is not adequate; companies they work for should *integrate* CSR strategically across their business models. This echoes the GVV conception of normality—values considerations should be a management activity just like any other.

Purpose

This idea of integrating values at work, commitment to social and environmental sustainability, and other millennial proclivities leads us to consider *purpose*. When students and young professionals identify business as the profession through which they can share their skills and talents, managers have ambitious young energy on their hands. When asked why they are studying business, students rarely cite salary as their primary motivation[25]—these young people are passionate, thoughtful, and ambitious. How can managers most effectively translate their capacities and preferences into positive impact?

The GVV approach calls us to define professional purpose explicitly and broadly—allowing us to see values conflicts as an expected part of business, with costs and benefits just like any other occupational challenge. Millennials' expressed desire to align purpose with professional life is useful for them and for their organizations—it can be a sustainable competitive advantage in today's business context:

> For example, if we think of our purpose as doing well, pleasing our bosses, making a good living (or even a great living), then when we face values conflicts in the workplace, we will see our degrees of freedom narrowed by the desire to please those very individuals who may be presenting us with the values conflict. They are the ones who give us performance reviews and raises, or with whom we need to cooperate in order to accomplish our goals, or to whom we need to make the sale to meet a quota. We may feel we have little choice but to do what they ask. Of course, the pursuit of any goal—even a narrowly defined goal—can still be guided and disciplined by a set of commitments and rules. Even if we define our purpose narrowly as "doing well financially," we can still choose to be guided by a set of values and principles that determine how we feel comfortable and justified in doing so, but they may feel more like constraints within which we must operate rather than goals to which we aspire. If, however, we think of our purpose in a broader sense as building and being part of a company that is a respected corporate citizen—for example, providing valuable products or services to consumers, creating good jobs in a healthy work environment, building a firm that investors can trust to report honestly on its performance—then we will see that we have a broader span of operation when we confront values conflicts. We will have a wider set of positive principles and goals to which we can refer and by which we can guide our behavior.[26]

This is a prosocial conception of purpose and one that aligns clearly with millennials and their goals. Of course it is also not the exclusive domain of young professionals. All of us can frame professional purpose broadly and explicitly and thus take steps toward building and sustaining organizations of which we can be proud.

Importantly, this broader definition of purpose should not lead us to infer that values conflicts are easy; rather, it may complicate matters because it requires us to see choices where we may have previously deferred to the "authority" of our superiors in the organization.[27] What this broader definition allows, however, is recognition of our efficacy and dignity at any level within an organization—we are part of something valuable that matters, as entry-level employees and as the CEO. We can "lead from any chair." This approach is reflected in increasing attention to collaborative organizations with flat rather than hierarchical structures.[28] This model resonates strongly with the strengths and preferences of millennials, and is the emerging model of today's business. Companies must develop a broad array of leaders, not simply a select few. We should also note here empirical research supporting the idea that millennials desire to contribute, express comfort with interaction with those in authority positions, and desire to be taken seriously as contributing members of the group.[29] We will discuss these implications in Chapters 4 and 6.

Additionally, millennials, those who follow Generation X, have been called "Generation Y"—alternatively, "Gen Why"—for good reason. They were taught that the context and significance of our actions matter and that there is something to be learned in everything they do.[30] They want to know how their contribution fits with the whole—this information on the "*why*" of what we do in our organizations must be communicated clearly and consistently for effective millennial engagement, and to the benefit of all workers and their managers. In Chapter 5 we explore this notion of purpose.

Self-Knowledge and Alignment

As we consider values and purpose, we must start with self-awareness. As young professionals and those who manage them consider their role and impact on their organizations, we can consider fostering values-based decision making. All managers have an interest in developing young talent who can contribute to effective, ethical organizations. To consider ethical judgment and action, we must explore the precursor of values identification—*What do I value? What do I believe should be done?*

Various exercises are available to explore personal and professional goals and our approaches to implement them, including comfort with risk, preferences in communication styles, and self-image. We include one of these tools, the "Personal-Professional Profile,"[31] as Appendix B. When we explore these inclinations we can more effectively enable ethical action that is consistent with who we are. Organizations that create opportunities to engage in this self-reflection and values alignment signal and operationalize a proactive, strength-building approach to professional development. This may become easier and more common in business, because this introspection and self-efficacy may come more naturally to millennials who have been raised to express opinions, feelings, and recommendations in ways that previous generations generally were not. Channeled around values, this tendency can help provide a foundation for ethical behavior. More information on self-knowledge and alignment is included in Chapters 5 and 6.

Voice

The ideas of *how* and *why* we express ourselves are fundamental when considering millennials at work—just ask any of their managers. Research indicates that most of us, regardless of generational cohort, share goals for our lives—live comfortably, raise families, contribute, feel engaged—yet the manner in which these goals are expressed and manifest at work can vary tremendously. Therein exists a major challenge. If we step back and consider "voice" at work—what we believe, and how we express what we believe—we can find useful insights.

Managers can consider exploring these topics with young talent, and with multigenerational employees throughout the organization, to root professional development in a commitment to values-based decision making at work. Tools for this approach are available. When we consider an exercise such as "Tale of Two Stories"[32] ("Action Item," this chapter, and Appendix A), or in any reflection of our professional selves, we can recognize occasions when we successfully acted in accordance with what we believed to be right, and episodes when we were unsuccessful. The factors that influenced the outcome—self-inflicted (rationalizations, short-term thinking) or other-related (pressure from superiors, expedience)—can, in many ways, be managed. Further, strategies adopted for resolving ethical issues within the organization, as opposed to externally (i.e., whistle-blowing), vary tremendously. We will discuss some of these reasons and rationalizations, and enablers to help managers and their millennial workers to confront them, later in this volume. But key at this point is the recognition that there are many different ways to speak. Thus, we can acknowledge: (1) that there are many ways to express values at work, and some are more effective in certain contexts than in others, (2) that all of us may be more skillful at, or more likely to use, one approach over another, (3) that some organizational conditions, and types of leaders within these contexts, will have a strong likelihood on our and others' likelihood of expressing values, and (4) that there are things millennials and their managers can do to make it more likely that we will voice our values effectively.[33]

Thus, these realities of expressing ourselves at work have tremendous implications for millennials and their managers. Research on leadership and organizational behavior indicates consistently that structure and style of our communication clearly influence outcomes. If managers desire behavior in accordance with shared values and organizational goals, we must think strategically about our organizational policies, processes, approaches, expectations—our organizational culture. We discuss this topic further in Chapters 3 and 6.

Reasons and Rationalizations

Managers (and most of us) are quite concerned with exploring the question, *Why do people behave unethically?* Research tells us that most of us consider ourselves to be ethical people, and most of us want to act in accordance with what we believe is right. Millennials and their managers, like all of us, can enhance professional impact by strengthening our resolve toward ethical behavior. Emerging research provides some answers as to why we fail to act on our values. Barriers to action—*reasons and rationalizations*—challenge our best attempts to achieve personal and organizational purpose.[34] Despite noble intentions, we may act unethically, we overestimate our ability to act ethically, and we are vulnerable to dynamics such as ethical fading, through which ethical dimensions are eliminated from decision making.[35] These barriers can be self- or other-imposed. Fortunately, we can consider categories of argument and rationalization, along with categories of values dilemmas, to help us recognize them, understand the ways of thinking that produce them, and to be practiced in responding to them. We can explore common barriers to ethical action by industry and job function. With explicit attention, they can become expected and normalized, and we can acknowledge that they are susceptible to reasoned response.

Thus, what are these reasons and rationalizations for behavior that is counter to our values, and how can we persuasively respond to them? How can managers create space for consideration of these critical professional issues? Young professionals seem to want to do what they think is right, and they need the skills necessary to communicate persuasively around values at work. Understanding the reasons and motivations for why we behave as we do—and why others behave as they do—helps us all become more effective at work. Further discussion of these strategies appears in Chapters 6 and 7.

Rethinking Ethics at Work

GVV incorporates an innovative and actionable premise. GVV founder Mary Gentile describes the process of developing the approach by imagining a bell curve: "At one tail-end of the bell curve . . . are people who would self-identify as opportunists, people who would say, "I will do whatever it takes to maximize my material self-interest, values be damned." Now, those people do exist. . . . And at the other end of the tail we'll say, "These are the people who would self-identify as idealists." Now, nobody fits into any of these categories all the time. It is often the perspective. But idealists would say, "I will always try to act on my values regardless of the impact on my material self-interest." *What we say is the majority of the people in the business school classroom . . . and the majority of people in business . . . are under the bell, and we call them pragmatists.* We define pragmatists as people who would say, "I would like to act on my values as long as it doesn't put me at a systematic disadvantage." Now, that's not the same as saying "as long as I know I will succeed"; it's not the same as saying "as long as I know I won't lose." It means "I think I might have a shot." So if you think of people that way, then our task as educators or as managers [changes]. . . . We don't have a lot of leverage with the opportunists, frankly. I'm not so worried about the idealists, except I wish they were more skillful and more competent. But I think *our leverage is with the pragmatists*. I think our leverage is with these folks who say, "I'd like to act on my values if I thought I had a shot." What we say is, "Well, let's give you the skills, the tools, and, importantly, the practice, to feel more equipped, so that you feel that you have more options, so that you feel like you can be more likely to succeed. . . . We're trying to help you be who you want to be at your best." So that's where we're focusing [with GVV]. That's where we feel that we may have some leverage. You know, the opportunists will always be with us. The point is you don't need everyone to behave perfectly. You need enough."[36]

Chapter 1: Action Item

"A Tale of Two Stories"

Readers are encouraged to engage with this book; future chapters will include key highlights from each topic to consider implementing in our own organizations. This first chapter includes an "Action Item" that allows us to put into practice the idea of implementing our values.

The exercise is a foundational GVV activity that has been used successfully with corporate and academic audiences. Managers can facilitate the exercise with their direct reports as the focus of a workshop, or it can be integrated into existing training and professional development programs. Additionally, millennial readers (or their managers) can consider the exercise as a tool for self-reflection.

The goal is to consider specific instances when the participant acted in accordance with what he/she believed to be right, and when he/she was not successful in acting on his/her values. Individual and group versions are included, and are readily adaptable for independent exploration or for a group development activity facilitated by a manager or other team member.

Our values and their impact on workplace decision making are part of daily professional life. Thinking explicitly about what we value, and our individual strengths and challenges around acting on them, is a helpful place to begin.

Chapter 1: Action Item

Exercise: A Tale of Two Stories

The exercise can be completed individually, or as part of training and development facilitated by a manager or group leader. If used as a group exercise, please see Appendix A for Facilitator Guide/Reflection Debrief.

In your careers thus far, you have likely encountered workplace situations when your values conflicted with what you experienced, observed, or were asked to do. Often it is not easy to align your own personal values and purpose with those of your boss, your coworkers, your direct reports, or your firm.

This exercise is designed to help you identify and develop the competencies necessary to achieve that alignment.

Objectives

(1) To reflect on your previous experiences, successful and less so, at effectively voicing and acting on your values in the workplace.

(2) To discover which conditions and problem definitions empower you to effectively voice your values, and which tend to inhibit that action.

Instructions[37]

Part I

- Recall a time in your work experience when your values[38] conflicted with what you were expected to do in a particular,

---

This material has been included with permission from the *Giving Voice to Values* curriculum collection, www.GivingVoicetoValues.org and www.MaryGentile.com, developed by Mary C. Gentile. The Aspen Institute was founding partner, along with the Yale School of Management, and incubator for *Giving Voice to Values* (GVV). Now Funded by Babson College.

nontrivial management decision, and you spoke up and acted to resolve the conflict.

- Consider the following four questions and write down your thoughts and brief responses:
  - What did you do, and what was the impact?
  - What motivated you to speak up and act?
  - How satisfied are you? How would you like to have responded? (This question is not about rejecting or defending past actions but rather about imagining your ideal scenario.)
  - What would have made it easier for you to speak/act?
    - Things within your own control
    - Things within the control of others

Part II

- Recall a time in your work experience when your values conflicted with what you were expected to do in a particular, nontrivial management decision, and you did *not* speak up or act to resolve the conflict.
- Consider the following four questions and write down your thoughts and brief responses:
  - What happened?
  - Why didn't you speak up or act? What would have motivated you to do so?
  - How satisfied are you? How would you like to have responded? (This question is not about rejecting or defending past actions but rather about imagining your Ideal Scenario.)
  - What would have made it easier for you to speak/act?
    - Things within your own control
    - Things within the control of others

CHAPTER 2

Always On: Technology & Voice

We begin with a discussion of how we can utilize technology to enhance the employment experience for managers and their teams, specifically in the realm of ethical impact. As we consider "voice" at work—whether, and the ways in which employees and their managers express themselves— we must explore one of the most salient issues of today's workforce: social media. We will focus on this water in which millennials swim as well as other opportunities for embracing technology toward organizational effectiveness.

Millennials use social media—a lot! In addition to using these tools to connect with one another, millennials talk publicly and often about their work, the resources they are using, their progress, and the challenges that arise. For better (and sometimes worse), this sharing, or "work narration" on blogs and other social networks, becomes part of their organizations' digital records.[39] Managers may immediately view this phenomenon with concern. Clear expectations around use of these technologies are critical. Yet, ultimately these tendencies can enhance organizational effectiveness. This "digital trail" can enhance efficiencies and create opportunities for dialogue.[40] With explicit attention, this form of voice can be channeled toward organizational development, and millennial comfort and fluency with technological voice may prompt innovative approaches to voicing values and new ideas within the organization. This addition to the organization's digital record and its processes—when managed well—can add to efficiencies and learning from others.

Harnessing the Power of Social Media

Much has been written about channeling technological capacities in a positive way toward organizational communication, branding, event, or product marketing. These skills clearly align with young professionals' interests and talents. "Millennials prefer quick results and find life easier by using Google rather than a dictionary. . . ."[41] This fluency extends to all areas of work. Thus, "the best way to get around an issue is to use it to your advantage. . . . Use the technologies that engage these individuals, and invest in them."[42] Social media can be utilized in two broad ways—as a means to connect with one another, and as a platform for distributing content, knowledge, and information. These technologies are also inherently team-centric—they involve interactive, collaborative communication as opposed to one-on-one, face-to-face connections—which may be particularly useful for millennials with their penchant for team orientation.

Of course social media and the ubiquitous access to technology can be misused. Social media use in highly regulated sectors like finance, for example, can be a legal minefield:

[For example,] Goldman [Sachs'] communications are scrutinized by an alphabet soup of state and federal regulators to ensure investors enjoy a level playing field. All activity—every last post, tweet, check-in, and poke related to business—must be recorded and archived. Firms can be held liable for tweets fired off from an employee's iPhone, outside the office, and after working hours. Even something as innocuous as clicking the Like symbol next to a Facebook post could run afoul of the SEC.[43]

Sectors other than financial services also face explicit regulations, of course, and companies may be underestimating some of the challenges due to the rapid spread of these technologies. As one strategist notes, "Go to LinkedIn and do a search for people currently employed by your enterprise . . . You will likely see thousands of them . . . without any compliance process or technology in place."[44]

Our corporate survey of over 60 executives from a variety of industries also reflected this concern about misuse and sharing of proprietary information, or information that reflects poorly on the company brand (note to millennial: do not post photos of yourself imbibing, wearing your corporate-logoed polo!).

Yet the news is not all bad. The best of our educational institutions are instilling this awareness in our graduates. Students responding to our survey of their perceptions reflected strong levels of recognition that it is inappropriate to compromise a corporate brand with negative imagery or narrative online. Yet reinforcement at the company is key. As we will explore in more detail below, a specific social media policy with clear and consistent guidelines for appropriate use is the responsibility of an effective and engaged management team. Inviting the perspectives of those most fluent in these technologies in the design of these policies can be invaluable. There are also many models of such policies available via a simple internet search. Companies can adapt the policies to suit their industry and specific needs.

Implementing a social media compliance process is manageable and effective. Start with a clear and specific policy, with the best of these reflecting collaboration—employees provide case examples from the front lines of the company, marketing determines the scope of messaging, IT outlines the technologies and devices, and the legal department ensures consistency with regulatory criteria. The next step is training and reinforcing the policy, and finally, some companies might consider specialized tools that monitor these types of communications.[45] As multiple cases illustrate, the alternative to these approaches, namely banning social communications altogether and hoping for compliance, is not feasible. "Restricting communication, access to information and people networks is something I doubt you would champion as a sound business practice for the 21st century. . . . You can resist, but your competitors and customers are moving ahead."[46] A recent report from Cisco reminds us that companies should embrace social networks effectively, rather than fear or attempt to eradicate them:

> One in three college students and young employees under the age of 30 would prioritize device flexibility and social media freedom over salary in accepting a job offer. In fact, 40 percent of college students and 45 percent of young employees said they would accept a lower-paying job that had more device flexibility and social media access, than a higher-paying job with less flexibility. . . . More than half of college students globally (56%) said that if they encountered a company that banned access to social media, they would either not accept a job offer *or would join and find a way to circumvent corporate policy.*[47] (emphasis mine)

This same report reiterated the importance of proactive social media in recruiting, training, and managing young talent—these techniques are positively associated with retention and engagement of top performers. By providing clear expectations about use by employees, and, more importantly, bringing millennial talent into the fold of development and management of these tools, we are channeling these tendencies in a positive way. Millennials are encouraged to use their talents in ways that benefit the organization, and thoughtful attention is paid to encourage ethical and positive use of the technologies toward shared goals.

Voice and Transparency

This proactive incorporation of technology is a manner of encouraging "voice"—whether, and the ways we speak out—toward ethical leadership. Particularly in this era of the transparency of the internet, we can consider the difference between expressing "voice" internally versus public sharing, or even whistleblowing. Employees who are part of a culture that encourages dialogue, considers respectful debate, and allows for "speaking up" are far less likely to turn outward. Cultures that allow and encourage voice are able to adapt and change in ways that allow for financial and reputational sustainability. When deconstructing the path toward disaster of almost every major corporate scandal brought to light by a whistleblower, we see moments when intervention by responsible management could have prevented major harm to many stakeholders, including the firms themselves. Corporate cultures that encourage voice could render whistleblowing unnecessary.

This internal resolution of ethical concerns is responsible business. Clearly there are circumstances when whistleblowing is appropriate. Ethicist DeGeorge (2009) offers helpful considerations. In essence, whistleblowing sets the loyalty an employee has to third parties against the loyalty he or she has to her employer—requiring us to consider when it is permissible and when it is obligatory. DeGeorge suggests that internal resolution is almost always preferable—recognizing that although there can be occasions when this is inappropriate, in general, employees should make good-faith efforts to work within firms toward positive change and to minimize any potential harm to all parties.[48] In addition, allowing for "speaking up" creates a climate where diversity of thought is encouraged, innovation is possible and creativity is embraced. As millennials ascend to leadership roles in business, perhaps we will see this dynamic of cultivating positive change through voicing values—even when it means raising questions or expressing dissent—embraced more readily.

The comfort with expressing "voice" that may come naturally to millennials is associated with their use of technology. Social networking is changing the game for companies—the frequency of use is a challenge and an opportunity. A growing number of employees spend some of their workday connected to one or more social networks, and young talent will continue to support this trend—according to a recent national survey, at this point, more than 1 in 10 employees are "active social networkers" who spend at least 30 percent of their workday linked up to one or more networks.[49] Our own research indicates that over half of the business students we surveyed engage with three or more different social media platforms *daily*.

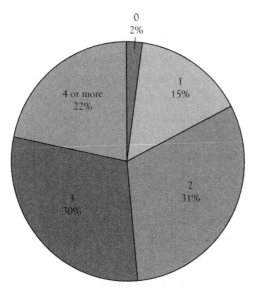

Figure 2.1 How many different social media platforms do you engage with daily? (n = 138)

The national study recognized both the challenges and potential of this new reality. Thus,

> Social networkers are clearly breaking old barriers and talking more freely than ever about their jobs and their company. They say they think about the risks before posting online and consider how their employers would react to what they post, but social networkers, and active social networkers in particular, do air company linen in public. . . . Workplace "secrets" are no longer secret, and management must assume that anything that happens at work, any new policy, product, or problem, could be publicly known at almost any time.[50]

This new transparency creates new management concerns. But the risks are manageable—clear policies, training about the use of social networks, and an ongoing commitment to an ethical culture in which employees act with integrity can mitigate these risks.[51] The key is proactive attention. When policies are in place and training is explicit, the content

of social media posts changes. Additionally,
that they are enthusiastically willing to use the
advocate for their companies.

Most successful large firms already use these
services and products, community engagement
awareness. But this attention should be inward-
ensure sustainable business success. "Creative businesses can also use social
networking to their advantage in terms of workplace ethics, using it internally to reinforce company values and build workforce loyalty and cohesion. . . . Build[ing] trust in managers . . . and inform[ing] and educat[ing]
employees on ethics issues that arise at work."[52] The benefits of these internal or enterprise social networks can include reduced communication
costs, increased employee engagement, collaboration, and innovation, and
they can bridge the gap between formal and informal learning, and lead
to increased business performance and enhanced competitive advantage.[53]

A report produced by professional services firm Deloitte notes that
applying "social software" can help companies generate tangible results:

> As the organization builds confidence and proficiency using social
> software, it can expand use of the tool to address additional attrac-
> tive opportunities where the potential impact and the employee
> engagement are high. Companies can reap significant financial
> rewards and develop skills and experience that have the potential
> to help them build a stronger competitive position over time.[54]

Using social media to enhance efforts toward engaged, connected employees resonates well with millennial abilities and interests and contributes to a culture of transparency and shared values. These young people
can help develop and grow these tools.

But this potential is unrealized—less than half of all respondent companies in a survey of over 2,000 professionals nationwide use social networking to assist senior leadership in communicating company values, to
build trust in managers, and to inform and educate employees on ethical
issues that may arise at work.[55] This finding was echoed in our own survey of corporate managers, with 47 percent reporting use of social media

y and 53 percent indicating no use of such technologies to con-
employees together and with management. For those in our study
whose companies do use such technologies, platforms included dedicated
Facebook pages, Yammer (an enterprise social networking tool for use
within individual businesses), Google tools, Twitter, YouTube, and internally managed wellness tools such as NOVU. Effective use of these
tools was also a concern. One of the minority of managers reporting use
of social media at work noted that these technologies were used, "but
badly. The people providing the content don't really know how to do so
in a timely manner, so it's a lost opportunity." This finding was echoed
several times.

Involving millennials in the design and implementation of these
social media policies and platforms is invaluable. Not only will buy-in
increase, but these young people can help managers navigate the ever-
changing technologies and tools. What worked in the past can quickly
become obsolete and less-than engaging. Without input from young
professionals, we run the risk of implementing social media approaches
that will be underutilized and ineffective. Several young people in our
study shared examples of unsuccessful attempts at technological connection by companies at which they were employed. These were typically
characterized as "top-down," required, and thrust-upon employees with
no incorporation of feedback on design and use; they were not seen as
meaningful nor were they used in any significant way. Unfortunately for
us non-millennials, by the time these technologies make their way across
our desks, the young people have moved on. Consider the MySpace
(remember that?) and Facebook phenomena, described by one of our
millennials thus:

> [Facebook] was the first big social media [tool] that I used so
> I experimented with it a bit, figuring out what you can put on
> there like your bios and all of the other features. Then once it
> got popular with people who were significantly older, like my
> grandma and my parents and aunts and uncles, I stopped using
> it regularly. I still have some information up there—you can't
> not be "friends" with your grandma—but it's not [something I
> regularly use].

Enhancing Ethical Cultures with Social Media

Ethical cultures can be reinforced through these tools. A national study of social networking in business provides specific suggestions.[56] Thus, strategies and social networking policies should be grounded in ethics and values and not merely compliance—the environment is continually changing and employees must be able to handle new situations with ethical implications. Additionally, social networking policies should be established from the outset, and should be reinforced with training to reduce risks for employees and for management. Rules must be rooted in reality to reflect the ways people actually interact with these technologies. Social networking should be used to the company's advantage for internal and external communications and outreach to employees, including content that reinforces the company's ethical culture. Finally, social networkers themselves should help shape the policy and help the ethics and compliance teams engage employees through social networking.

Assuming that transparency is essential for today's sustainable businesses, management must acknowledge that just about anything that occurs could become public. This does not mean airing dirty laundry; rather, proactive and consistent attention to these dynamics mitigates risk by creating a culture of integrity that will make risk management pro- rather than reactive. Another tip is involving managers in direct and regular discussion with their reports around these issues—this explicit and ongoing interaction, favored by millennials, fosters an ethical culture of engaged employees.

Technology for Training and Engagement

Research indicates other specific techniques for engaging millennials around effective use of technology. Thus, of course, "computers are not ends in themselves" and technology is not a substitute for instruction and training; however, they can absolutely enhance learning outcomes and success.[57] Blogs, gamification (computerized simulations and role plays), collaborative learning and discussion portals (i.e., Google Docs), Twitter and related tools, and wikis (open access [or relatively open—these can be managed within the company] information gateways) are several approaches. Incorporating the GVV tenets of voice and peer coaching can be helpful here. Peer coaching, or opportunities to consider workplace challenges interactively with colleagues, can be used to consider technology concerns at work. Through training and development activities, managers and discussion facilitators can propose ethical dilemmas around technology issues and participants can develop and practice "scripts" for addressing them. This allows for engaging and action-oriented consideration of issues likely to arise in the specific context of the organization. Participants then "coach" one another on enhancing the responses to best reflect corporate policy to develop realistic and implementable solutions. It is a collaborative and hands-on, action-oriented approach, which resonates well with millennials:

> Insightful and supportive peer feedback on discussants' proposed "scripts" and strategies for responding to values conflicts is an essential part of the *Giving Voice to Values* approach. . . . [T]hose who share their proposed responses to the values conflict, as well as those who are serving as "peer coaches," all adopt a stance of joint problem solving. That is, the role of the coaches is not to "grade" their peers' responses, but rather to work as a team to enhance them. This includes noting the strengths of a proposed response (so that they can be retained) as well as identifying the remaining questions (so that the group can collaborate on more effective solutions).[58]

Benchmarking best practices in social media compliance, considering cases that illustrate potential challenges at work, and discussion of responses are all opportunities for managers to engage their teams around such issues. Using these mechanisms to generate examples of ethical decision making at work reinforces and motivates good behavior, and also triggers the collaborative, team-oriented, peer and aspirational leader motivation millennials appreciate. This focus is clearly consistent with leveraging millennial interest and talent toward organizational effectiveness.

Additional suggestions might include gamification of training and development materials, engaging employees with short, frequent, and positive communications around values (for example, through case exercises or videos), supporting technology for employees and your stakeholders (consumers and investors use these tools as well!), and providing innovative access points such as apps and accessible internet presence—and, as noted above, these approaches can be designed and managed by young talent to enhance the organizational effectiveness of all.

"Gamification" has been noted as a strategy for training and development and its rise merits consideration here. "Serious games" or simulations that include elements of games such as stories, goals, feedback, and play allow for experiential learning, skill reinforcement, supplemental instruction, access opportunities for practice, and increasing contact with content in a learning environment.[59] Early adopters of these technologies report satisfaction with engagement and learning outcomes. Careful and deliberate use of these approaches can be effective with millennial talent and impactful across the organization. Resistance is clearly an issue for more traditional managers—one respondent in our survey of corporate leaders noted that *"social media does not belong in the workplace—work is not play!"* For these technologies to be useful, they must be managed. These tools must be framed explicitly to acknowledge the distinction between resources that incorporate elements of gaming, and "games" that may carry implications that are not optimal for values discussions. Providing evidence of the connection between engagement with such tools and enhanced learning outcomes is key. Clarifying the distinction between "gamification" and simply "games" means acknowledging that the former focuses on cognitive processes and tries to bring what we know about effective engagement into the learning environment. Gamification can be associated with enhanced intrinsic motivation and memory, and with greater engagement and attention to the learning content.[60,a]

---

[a]*Giving Voice to Values* offers an optional mobile and social learning tool called @GVV which aligns well with the digital environment in which today's professionals operate. Participants learn through modular units that incorporate "web-based text, video, illustrations, quizzes, polls, debates and group projects" that allow learners to explore key concepts determined by the facilitator or manager as an extension of existing programs or as a stand-alone opportunity to reinforce learning. Nomadic Learning, "*Giving Voice to Values*," Mary C. Gentile.

Communicating Explicitly and Often

In today's workplace it is vital that employees feel connected. Technology is an efficient and effective way to keep people engaged—if it is meaningful, and if it represents multiple "voices," including fostering communication initiated by these young professionals. Empirical research found that those managers of all age groups who are deliberately redundant as communicators—communicating the same message over and over, via both face-to-face and technology such as e-mail and texts—are more successful at moving projects along faster and more smoothly than those who are not.[61] This millennial proclivity actually helps members of all generations work more productively. As we will discuss in Chapter 7, we also see benefits from prompting frequent retrieval of values and expectations among our employees to reinforce and operationalize ethical cultures. Additionally, as we will explore further in Chapter 4, scholars have found that manager-led or peer-to-peer mentoring at top companies, *including such approaches as online platforms,* leads to decreased training costs and enhanced communication.[62]

The connections between creation of ethical and productive cultures at work and communication through social networking are many, and the tools of the social network that reflect transparency, simplification, and amplification are vital for clearly and easily communicating expectations. The tools have enhanced our ability to document and describe our interactions and activities, which can be "a winning combination for organizing a shared behavioral context, establishing trust and motivating action. Contrast this with historical efforts to engender sustainable behavior change, which are often underpinned by factual content, yet delivered through opaque and largely symbolic formats devoid of personally relatable experiences."[63]

Further, setting these expectations around ethical cultures with emphasis on social and environmental sustainability of business, an increasingly critical concern, is within the province of millennials, and there remains much potential for development of this new paradigm. Social networking and attention to social and environmental sustainability have evolved rapidly over the last decade to emerge as significant drivers of social change, and both are largely produced and consumed by millennials.[64]

Social Media and Social Activism

We can consider the myriad ways social media has been used to promote positive change in the areas of activism and global connectedness—shining a light on unethical practices, providing a mechanism for communicating and connecting, crowd funding social causes, and mobilizing change. Companies can get out in front of these trends rather than merely react, often when it is too late. Managers can lead the way in integrating social changes in ways that align with their specific company's mission and that leverage existing resources to channel these social commitments into impactful solutions with shared values. Our corporate survey results indicate strong manager perceptions of this social and environmental awareness among young talent. Yet this passion can be enhanced by channeling it in ways that create shared value and impactful solutions. Translating this awareness into action may be untapped potential for many businesses. As one of our corporate executives noted, *"We can do more [in the area of social and environmental awareness]. [Millennials] are aware of the issues but move on quickly to the next thing without necessarily sticking with it long enough for long term solutions."*

I have witnessed this phenomenon of fleeting attention in my own classrooms. For example, a recent episode of this "viral activism" occurred en masse during the Kony 2012 Invisible Children incident. A quick background: a compelling video purporting to expose Joseph Kony, the guerrilla leader of a Ugandan rebel movement, his atrocities, and the failure of authorities to contain him, began making the rounds among college students and other young people seemingly overnight in March 2012. The video was covered by news outlets from NPR to the Washington Post but most interestingly, it was a movement birthed by the internet. The YouTube upload of the video received over *43 million views* in 72 hours, and "sharing" the link on Facebook and other tools was rampant. By the time I had seen the new coverage, of course, my young students had already heard all about it. In classes, we discussed the issue and its salience among social media users. Nearly all of my students had viewed the video. The debate in the public sphere was fascinating. "Invisible Children" has since come under fire for incomplete coverage of a nuanced topic, and while there is broad agreement about the atrocities, a concern was that the video was misleading in some of its details. A more important concern, in my opinion, is what the episode vividly illustrated about the power and implications of social media for activism. Many students knew very little about the issue beyond what they had seen in the clip, and most did not actively seek out confirmation or more detail. They were confident spreading the clip to others without independent verification.

At this writing, the "ice bucket challenge" phenomenon is spreading as participants douse themselves (and, of course, videotape and upload the footage to the internet) and challenge others to do the same, purportedly in the name of ALS ("Lou Gehrig's Disease") charities. Footage of celebrities and others undertaking the "challenge" is making the rounds at warp speed. A criticism that is beginning to emerge, however, is whether participants know the mission behind the meme, or are contributing to the cause in any meaningful way. While money raised for a worthy cause is certainly nothing to lament, a concern might be the dynamics that the episode illustrates—fleeting attention for social commitment, dilution (pardon the pun) of core social missions, lack of understanding and sustainable contributions—awareness should be a precursor to an engagement, not the end itself.

What are the implications of these phenomena for the workplace? Perhaps we can consider how this awareness can translate into action, particularly in collaboration with efforts in corporate social responsibility. At best, these internet memes can raise awareness and prompt further exploration of critically important issues, often generated by those without access to traditional means of engaging with others. Of course, around the world, social media has played an instrumental role in movements for positive social change and freedom. A concern, however, is that these viral video phenomena may promote a type of token engagement that promotes self-satisfaction on the part of the "activist" with no true commitment to understanding, dialogue, or problem solving involved—activism is as simple as clicking a "like" button. Opportunities for meaningful engagement in complex issues may be lost. Many of my students felt moved by the Kony video movement and considered it thoughtfully. Most, however, had moved on by the time I revisited the topic in class shortly after the story reached the traditional news media. So can we build on this energy more fruitfully, perhaps through the institution of business, with its reach and scale—its tremendous potential for impact?

Committed young people, educators and managers can channel these passions and interests from fleeting concerns to the pursuit and realization of actionable solutions. Millennials have their fingers on causes that matter and on issues that engage their counterparts. The business community can have a positive impact on urgent social needs through efforts ranging from cause-related marketing to strategic alliances between corporations and social movements. Managers can institutionalize solutions that align with corporate purpose.

One illustrative new approach that signals the willingness of corporations to use technological tools in innovative ways—and that recognizes the scale and urgency of global social issues demands new models based on collaboration—is a new tool called Collectively, a nonprofit venture launched by corporate giants (and rivals) Coca-Cola, PepsiCo, Unilever, and Nestle, among 29 others. Collectively is a digital hub designed to inspire collective action by young people around climate change. "Collectively will connect millennials to the innovations that are shaping the future, making it easy for them to act, buy, invest and promote the ideas that they believe in. To be part of the solution."[65] Through stories and information highlighting innovations, the goal is to connect passions with information and opportunities for engagement.

We will discuss these ideas of individual and corporate purpose further in Chapter 5. Yet the link between social networking and these issues is important. Companies are encouraged to foster sustainable business cultures by cultivating the gifts of millennial talent. These young influencers can be enabled to promote and share specific solutions within their networks. Companies interested in promoting ethical causes can work with these passionate young people to spread the word and motivate action—"socially networked millennials could just be our best bet for positive action toward sustainable future."[66]

Social Media for Recruiting and Connecting Employees

In this globalized work environment, connectedness via social media can be invaluable. Channeling this proclivity during the transition from college to the workplace can have real impact on our young employees.

Research tells us "as organizations embrace a team approach to address an increasingly competitive global business environment, higher education must provide students the skills necessary to succeed in team-oriented business environments"; further, "better knowledge, understanding and application of how social media technologies can support group work could enhance the ability of individuals to work collaborative in remote teams, an increasingly important requirement in today's workplace."[67] Anecdotal and empirical evidence illustrates the increasingly diverse nature of our companies.[68] Because of technology (webcams, virtual conferencing, and so on), we have increased collaboration among diverse participants. This is unequivocally good for business.

An additional note on technology as a critical consideration merits attention. As companies work to design effective recruitment and retention strategies for millennials, and all employees, the transparency the internet provides raises the stakes dramatically. Candidates and employees are well aware of those companies identified as "best to work for," and of policies and practices of individual companies.[69] Current and former employees can "narrate" their work experiences for all to see. Managers would do well to acknowledge the accessibility of this information. It clearly impacts job seekers—and, of course, other corporate stakeholders including consumers, investors, employees, competitors, and others—and must be managed well. Millennial employees, with their fluency and skill in these domains, can be an asset to proactive companies seeking to manage their online presence. Effective engagement with social media platforms, and monitoring of stakeholder perceptions and other techniques are squarely within the domain of millennial workers and can be leveraged toward organizational success.

This technology can enhance every stage of the employment experience. New models are emerging all the time. Online shoe retailer and perennial example of engaging corporate culture Zappos.com recently made headlines[70] when it announced that it would no longer post job openings, in favor of a truly networked alternative. Their social network, "Zappos Insiders," will serve as a place for employees and fans to interact and will allow management to cultivate their talent pool and connect with candidates—interested job seekers must join the network and participate in digital discussions and Q&As—the employer will use new technology to sort candidates into functional area "pipelines" and hire through the site. The *Wall Street Journal* notes,

> In some ways, Zappos can seem less like a shoe retailer than an experiment in how a company can be run. Chief Executive Tony Hsieh has confessed in media interviews to having a 'negative interest' in shoes and has set a corporate goal to 'create fun and a little weirdness.' The company also practices holacracy, a management system that rejects hierarchy and instead spreads authority and decision making evenly across an organization.[71]

With these and other innovations that resonate well with today's top talent, it is not surprising that Zappos makes regular appearances on "best company to work for" lists.

Scholars also recognize that it is not perks alone, like colorful workplaces and workout rooms, which attract millennial talent. A professor of systems thinking notes,

> Companies such as Zappos, Google, and Microsoft have become destinations for young workers not just because of their attractive salaries and benefits, but because they created collaborative offices and pushed their companies' social ethos. . . . Managers should take note, and motivate workers by stressing the social value of millennials' work. . . . As baby boomers, we learned the culture of the organization and played by the rules. Millennials are coming in and saying, 'This is what we value. This is what's important, and my commitment is not to the company but is [to] what they do.'[72]

The role of purpose at work is explored further in Chapter 5.

Several approaches to effectively manage young professionals resonate directly with the GVV principles of building ethical corporate cultures. For example, while suggested perks like collaborative office design, providing snacks, and casual dress days may certainly prove effective with millennial and other workers, and may in practice foster ethical cultures through shared experience and feelings of connectedness, other techniques offer immediate returns. Thus, modeling the sentiment that all workers are value-added colleagues from the start fosters a norm of mutual respect that can be expected from millennial workers in return.[73]

Networking Literacy and Implications for Training and Development

We can consider the new fluencies that the most successful millennials possess. This "networking literacy" involves interpreting and contributing to the vast trove of information online, navigating this information and using context and connections to make sense of it, and multitasking and focus literacy in this era of nonstop access.[74] Again we must acknowledge the ethical issues inherent in these connections. This communication capacity involves an unprecedented level of transparency and access, and millennials have known no other platform for social and market commerce.[75] From internet etiquette, both social and professional, to issues of loyalty, information privilege, and other implications, we are in a new era with new responsibilities for ethical management and decision making.

Best practices in facilitating professional development trainings can be effective for all the generations in our organizations by leveraging these millennial capacities around technology. Traditional classroom training, "blended learning" that incorporates web-based components, and online-only approaches can be enhanced in multigenerational workplaces. Suggestions for effective training[76] include:

- Embrace active "classrooms"—avoid the traditional leader-led, lecture approach to distributing contents.
- Establish credibility quickly and carefully.
- Include visual elements and use technology in an engaging way.
- Allow for blended learning that incorporates some content available "on demand."
- Provide young people opportunities to lead the group.
- Explain the "whys"—the big picture and significance.
- Ask for the opinions of those in the group.

Again, these strategies are not only effective for managing young professionals. Providing all participants with clear expectations for the training, and acknowledging the "why" of what we do, does not need to be restricted to manager–millennial communication. This attention to organizational purpose benefits all employees, and the company as a whole. The knowledge and content areas of the training can effectively be conveyed using technology. Delivery options ranging from online information portals to "serious gaming" can be employed effectively and with impact. Employee input, collaboration, feedback, and development can be transformational to traditional performance processes through the effective use of technology. Employers can consider various available approaches, and can enhance the culture of the organization through tools that help with engagement, connection, and transparency. Additional examples are provided in our discussion of corporate best practices in Chapter 7.

Companies benefit from transparency around their vision and practices, and their approaches to employee engagement are evident to job seekers early in the process. One business student shared his process of determining where to work:

> I had multiple offers from big four firms and [many students at this point find it] hard to differentiate between the firms. . . . For me it really came down to the type and degree of communication I had with my contacts there, and how comfortable I felt with them. It really came down to who I could see myself working with at 10 or 11 o'clock at night in a team room and not want to just kill the other person. You really have to think about where you can see yourself and what kind of culture you picture yourself in.

Another student remarked, "I really look for the culture of helping each other out and showing they're investing in you with mentors and coaches. . . . I'm willing to work like a dog [if they invest in me]."

Multitasking and Community

A final note on technology merits mention. Because the GVV approach is inherently behavior- and action-oriented, it requires a level of contextual and self-awareness. In this era where we are "always on," we must acknowledge the relationship between mindfulness and multitasking. Some interesting questions arise for managers concerned about ethical culture at work. When we multitask, are we capable of true collaboration, of empathy, of community? Socially networked communities may foster a false impression of context around norms and values. We are influenced by the conduct of others—thus, we must be intentional about creating communities in this new environment. To guard against context collapse, millennials and those who hope to engage with them successfully must cultivate relationships and consensus around values and mission. Is the very nature of relationships changing due to social media? How can managers acknowledge both the relational aspect of millennial talent, and this new paradigm of social media environments?

A challenge these technologies present involves the potential dangers of one-sided communication. Companies may fear (and in some cases, justifiably) that social media "shining a light" on alleged unethical practices can result in misinformation to stakeholders if allegations prove unfounded—sometimes in a big way. Proactively managing online presence is a must for today's companies. Yet this "single stream" communication also has implications for our society more broadly. As social media tools become ever more concise, in some cases limited to 140 characters, and as images increasingly replace text to communicate ideas, this potential for risk increases. Consider one university student's appreciation for tools like Twitter because you can speak out without repercussion: *"You're less likely to get into an actual conversation with someone [then on other tools such as Facebook]"*. Another noted, *"What you tweet is straight out of your mouth."*

There is also the siren song of the anonymity of the internet to guard against; proactive attention to use of these technologies can reinforce their effective use and acknowledge that we must consider context and impact. Explicitly naming these concerns to young talent is encouraged. Students in our study, despite recognition of privacy considerations, still perceive a level of namelessness—with some even sharing that they post under pseudonyms. *"It's quicker, faster and easier to see what people think and are talking about."* The beauty of these tools is that they can cultivate transparency and collaborative interaction. Smart young people, such as one who remarked *"face to face conversations [must not be entirely replaced by electronic communication]. . . . Interaction and adjusting the conversation based on nonverbal queues is helpful in avoiding misunderstandings,"* recognize these tools as complements, not replacements for, traditional communication. Yet, potential for misuse of social media communication must be managed through policies and reinforcement at work. Broader implications for the future of communication in our society are a topic for another book!

A recent study from Rutgers University and Pew Research describes the "spiral of silence"[77] in which social media users may be less likely to share opinions if they run counter to prevailing thought expressed by others in their network. The implications for robust and principled debate of important issues are concerning. Encouraging the best of what social media has to offer—communications and connections, and "shining a light"—and guarding against its potential harm— discouraging thoughtful reflection—can be actively pursued by engaging young people in discussions of these issues, by exploring examples, and by considering their implications. Doing so in collaboration with peers and managers at work can be effective and engaging, and signal that these conversations are part of the new normal for professional life. Replacing dialogue with one-sided communication leaves us all sorely lacking. *"Too often we enjoy the comfort of opinion without the discomfort of thought."—John F. Kennedy*

Responsible Use

Responsibility for effective use of technology does not only rest with our companies. Millennials must proactively manage their online presence. "To navigate the new workplace. . . . millennials need to master a new set of rules that aren't taught in school. Advances in technology, the rise of social media, and 24/7 connectivity mean young people have to promote themselves and take ownership of their careers in ways that previous generations wouldn't or couldn't have imagined."[78] We discuss "personal branding" later in the book but in my experience teaching hundreds of these young people, they do acknowledge their responsibility here, and though we have engaged in passionate discussion about privacy and the blurring of boundaries between personal and professional identities, there is consensus around professionalism and good judgment. For example, emerging data suggest that millennials are more astute about protecting their individual data online than are members of other generations. Harris Interactive surveyed over 2,000 Americans on their online privacy habits and found that 78 percent of users aged 18 to 34 expressed a wish for privacy, compared to 59 percent of users 35 and up.[79] These results are consistent with those from other studies. The Pew internet and American Life project found that "the youngest social media users surveyed (those aged 18 to 29) are more likely to have cleared their browser histories, deleted or edited past social media postings, set their browsers to disable cookies, declined to use a website that required them to go by their real name, and employed a temporary username or e-mail address to hide their identity online. A 2007 Pew report found that among teenagers who use the internet, only 6 percent 'post their first and last names on publicly-accessible profiles.'"[80]

One of our survey respondents, echoing the remarks of several others, noted, *"We have grown up with these technologies. Our use [of these tools] allows us to be independent and creative."* Perhaps we have reason to be optimistic that millennials are becoming more thoughtful about responsible use.

From recruiting and hiring to professional development throughout the employment experience, practices can be enhanced through strategic use of technology. Thoughtful approaches can encourage worker interaction, accessibility, purpose, and engagement—these new instruments for voice can help us build stronger, more sustainable organizations.

Chapter 2: Action Items

Effective use of technology can enhance our organizations toward ethical impact, and millennial talent is poised to help make this happen. Below are key suggestions millennials and their managers can consider to maximize technological tools toward organizational goals.

(1) To manage privacy and appropriate use, to signal commitment to effective and collective use of technology toward organizational goals, and to mitigate risk, *develop a clear, specific, consistent and relevant policy around use of social media at work.* Clarify how and when information should be shared. Develop the policy collaboratively, involving multiple departments in design and implementation, and include millennials in development and ongoing management of the policy and its administration.

(2) *Train employees on the policy and provide opportunities for reinforcement, using engaging methods* such as group discussion of "live" case examples related to technology use at work. This has the dual benefit of providing examples and context for discussion of corporate values, including around issues of loyalty, diversity, privacy, and other ethical considerations prompted by social media use.

(3) *Use technology for connection and for sharing content—within and outside of your organization.* Inward-facing communication through social media can reinforce corporate values and build cohesion. External communication can engage stakeholders, including potential talent, and millennials can help drive this content to ensure that it is relevant and engaging.

(4) *Consider incorporating technology into training and development activities* to incorporate elements of "gaming" to include stories, goals, and feedback, and to engage employees and reinforce key concepts, including corporate mission and values-based decision making. Elements such as immediate feedback loops can engage employees at all levels of the organization in meaningful ways.

(5) *Encourage expression of voice through social media*—content can be generated by millennials, or others at work, and can provide discussion starters and information sharing. Post interesting news stories. Share accomplishments and highlights of the work experience. Foster connections among employees, and between employees and management, so that communication is meaningful and ongoing.

(6) *Engage millennial talent to enhance corporate involvement with social and environmental sustainability.* Encourage employees to acknowledge causes that matter to them, and consider building corporate partnerships and community engagement around these interests. Leverage millennial strengths including networking and communication to share stories and increase impact.

(7) *Recognize that information about our organizations is readily available to a variety of external constituents through these tools, and allow millennial employees to help manage the company's online presence.* Recruiting and retaining committed, bright, and values-oriented young professionals, and connecting with others, and with social impact and other opportunities that reflect shared goals, can be enhanced through this presence.

CHAPTER 3

Altogether, Now: Engagement & Multigenerational Workplaces

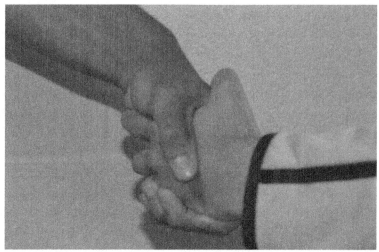

All photographs used with permission, Copyright © 2014 by Della Dewald

Next we turn to exploration of the changing nature of business, and the particular relevance of millennial skills and interests to this new space in which engagement and connections are critical. We will explore these characteristics, and consider how they can contribute to productive corporate cultures. Companies are increasingly relying on groups, teams, and multi-team systems to accomplish the complex tasks faced by the modern workplace.[81] Businesses are more connected and communicative, internally and externally, than ever before. These connections can be leveraged toward effective, ethical business, and collaboration is key. Thinking about our connections at work prompts consideration of "voice," or the ways in which we engage with one another around values, goals, objectives, and activities. Importantly, the decision to voice and act on values, both in accordance with personal goals defined individually, and with professional goals such as those defined by our organizations, can be enhanced through training and development.

Why does this consideration of voice matter and have particular resonance with millennial talent? We know that engaged and connected workplaces make for productive and successful companies. Millennial workers are motivated to contribute to the connected workplace, because we also know that millennials express an explicit desire for connections with peers and colleagues. This penchant can enhance economic viability. Research supports the idea of shared leadership, noting that long-term benefits accrue through more balanced, collaborative perspectives in leadership and decision making.[82] "Nearly every person is capable of taking on some leadership responsibility and positively contributing to organizational success. In this regard, knowledge should always trump status. . . . It is important for the organization to create an environment where every employee is encouraged to provide leadership, not simply those with the highest status or title."[83] These scholars also note the connections between responsible leadership, corporate social responsibility (CSR), effective teamwork, and productive organizations: "Shared leadership offers the potential to encourage responsibility at the core of the influence process through the naturally occurring balance that is fostered by spreading leadership throughout a workforce rather than centralizing it in the hands of a few formally designated leaders."[84] Not surprisingly, this approach is quite attractive to millennials, and it has been shown to enhance success across all levels of the organization. Thus, exploring these dynamics can be helpful for young professionals and their managers.

Shared decision making acknowledges that collaborative work is key, and this collaboration can begin between employee and manager. We discuss mentoring more specifically in Chapter 4, but for our purposes here it is important to acknowledge the foundation of the employee–manager relationship for engaged, collaborative, multigenerational cultures. Thus, we can consider another expressed desire of millennials at work—training and development, and regular and open feedback from their superiors. This desire for information exchange extends to matters typically reserved for more senior employees,[85] which, of course, has implications that are interesting for multigenerational cultures. Our task as managers is to influence these dynamics. If we emphasize developing one's skills and voice, in light of research that demonstrates that exchange of diverse ideas and analyses lead to enhanced creativity, opportunities, risk management strategies, and other benefits, we acknowledge that millennials' proclivity toward and comfort with dialogue—encouraged, open, ongoing and two-way—fosters organizational cultures that encourage leveraging our voices toward shared goals.

When we thoughtfully design and implement professional development at work, we can enhance learning and contribution by all employees toward shared goals and outcomes. Managers have a mandate to cultivate employee behavior to align with values and ethical standards of the organization. They can also foster new and further development of key issues within the company as identified by employees, who are increasingly expressing their commitments to ethical workplaces. Fostering a collaborative culture engages all levels of talent, allows for employee alignment with corporate goals, and encourages ownership and commitment toward enhancing the success of the firm.

Commitment to working together toward shared values can begin with considerations of motivation—*why* do we do what we do at work? A fundamental consideration, again reflected in the "Tale of Two Stories" provided in Chapter 1, explores why individuals choose to act, or not. This practice "voicing values" can be an invaluable part of professional development. Research indicates that a shared characteristic of those who act with moral courage in the face of confounding circumstances—gathered from situations as perilous as those faced by rescuers providing safety to those under Nazi threat during WWII—is prescripting, or anticipating values challenges and sharing, out loud, how to confront these challenges.[86] Again we see the roles here for professionals, both business people and academics in our business schools. Professional development that involves exploration of case studies, such as those provided in this volume, and "scripting" responses to ethical challenges, can be an effective approach. Determining mechanisms for practicing choice and developing our professional voice is the domain of business schools, and should be that of management as well.

We can consider another millennial phenomenon for clarity. We have all heard the frustration aimed at "helicopter parents" and perhaps lamented the state of "kids today" (as we simultaneously help our progeny complete their college applications with verve and polish). The culture of attention in which millennials were raised—these children of the baby boomers, let us remember who parented them!—is unprecedented. Those experiences of early and consistent intervention and feedback, with their corollary—the self-esteem-building focus where every child gets a trophy, for showing up and giving his or her best—can prove challenging as these young people enter a world rife with competition and little hand-holding.

It is unsurprising that these experiences translate into specific desires at work. Millennials expect not only frequent communication with supervisors, but that the communication be more positive and more affirming than has been the case with those in other generations.[87] Scholars posit that this need for affirmation develops from a constant flow of supportive messages from parents, teachers, and coaches during childhood. Perhaps we can understand, then, why young professionals may be struggling to reconcile the messages from their youth—*Reach for the stars! You can be whatever you want to be (and you'll be great at it)!*—with the current economic conditions and a business community that does not always seem to respond to this approach.

Toward Effective Engagement

Can we channel these tendencies in a positive way, rather than simply lamenting them? Collaborative cultures begin with communication. At even entry- and low-level positions, millennials express a need to be "kept in the loop" of information and expect that supervisors will freely share information such as strategic plans even during the formulation stage by senior management.[88] These tendencies have strong roots, thus, "as teens, [millennials] became comfortable expressing their thoughts and opinions to adults, expecting credibility despite their young age and lack of experiences. . . . They have also been encouraged by their parents to challenge authority, and to assert themselves, asking for preferential treatment when they believe they can get it."[89]

Therein lies the responsibility of our business schools, and of managers. We would do well to emphasize to young talent that increased engagement must be associated with increased responsibility. Experiential learning through internships and project-based learning are helpful approaches here and many business schools offer these opportunities as a core component of the curriculum. Modeling and providing opportunities for exercising this responsibility is critical for managers. It is worth it—research tells us that investing millennials with more and broader responsibilities can foster feelings of involvement, which in turn fosters organizational attachment and performance.[90]

The goal again becomes encouraging manager openness to millennial strengths, and its necessary corollary, enhancing millennials' appreciation for work relationships and respect for experience. Organizational openness can create a space in which frank communication and problem solving between millennials and their supervisors occurs.[91] Research indicates that consistent communication, regular feedback, and other engagement between supervisor and employee lead to enhanced organizational outcomes. We saw this finding reflected in our own millennial interviews, and as one that may be quite different than that of previous generations: *"I had two different internship experiences . . . [during one] I talked to my boss every single day, multiple times a day and I was getting constant feedback on how I was doing. . . . I always knew if I was doing a good job or what I could do differently. I enjoyed this much more."*

Developing and encouraging voice at work, which includes effective, constructive engagement around values and perspectives, can channel these characteristics. Further, because of the parenting millennials have often experienced, they clearly value and expect personal achievement. Managers can capitalize on this value toward organizational goals. These need not be resource-intensive. Techniques might include peer recognition of goal achievement and other means to incentivize performance toward shared goals. Acknowledging the role of institution-building in professional leadership development is another opportunity here. A natural place for fostering consensus is around values at work, including considerations of such questions as, *What is our firm's purpose? How can we meet our goals responsibly and sustainably?* Open and participatory communication on these issues can net important advantages for the company.

This task of building consensus and shared engagement is not easy. The oppositional nature of millennials and other age cohorts at work, and of young talent "versus" the establishment, is regularly highlighted in the media, such as this *Businessweek* feature:

> It's the fight of a generation. In this corner, weighing in at 42.5 million people, with a 12.3 percent unemployment rate and $294 billion of combined student loan debt, wearing skinny jeans and headphones: 20 to 29-year-olds. *And* in this corner, tipping the scale at 36.9 million people, with an unemployment rate of 6.6 percent and a median household net worth of $162,000, wearing Crocs and a pair of bifocals: 55 to 64-year-olds. Let's get ready to rumble.[92]

Of course, and as this article's author notes, more realistically millennials and baby boomers are not competing for the same jobs. But considering the relative status of each group can illustrate some of the respective challenges that may engender more *understanding and connection*. The economy matters for both. Young people with lower earning potential in their future than their elder peers, mounting student loan debt, and significantly higher unemployment rates (and the societal challenges we all face) are immediate concerns for millennials, while boomers struggle with relatively more damaging unemployment and shrinking retirement funds—our Businessweek author here ends with this less-than-optimistic quote: "Both [millennial and boomer] situations are terrible, but their problems are different."[93]

One student respondent noted his perception of a disconnect and misunderstanding:

> I think that there is a definite distinction between the work ethic of my generation and that of my grandparents. I think that the generalization that my entire generation is comprised of selfish, lazy, & entitled individuals is unfair. I have many peers who are quite the opposite. I think the problem that causes these perceptions is how drastically different the culture that these different

generations were born into. My generation seems to be more op
minded on social issues. . . . We were also born into a more stable
and very technologically advanced economy. I believe this greatly
impacts older generations' view of us millennials because the
concept of what constitutes work has greatly changed . . .. Instead
of looking for jobs, many of us are looking for callings. This is an
opportunity many members of older generations did not have. In
addition, with how quickly technology has evolved in the last 10
to 15 years our entire world has been changed. It is my generation
that has grown up with all of the technological advancements and
because of this I think it has impacted our way of problem solving
in that we instinctively tend to find solutions that involve technology as a way to minimize the necessary work for a result.

Focusing on shared values is more productive for all of us. My contention is that we share many values, and we simply manifest them differently. A study of generations and their values at work[94] found that
millennials, generation Xers, and baby boomers all shared the same top-
five expectations of their employers:

- challenging work;
- competitive compensation;
- opportunities for advancement, and chances to grow in their jobs;
- fair treatment;
- work–life balance.

This does not mean that cross-generational friction does not occur.
Rather, it reminds us of a useful starting point for organizational cohesion
and development. All employees can benefit from a culture that encourages proactive decision making and provides opportunity for development and growth. Here we can consider the *Giving Voice to Values* pillar
of emphasizing shared values for effective decision making. These values
can be a foundation to which we can appeal when trying to address values
conflicts. They allow us to consider effective strategies for pursuing shared
goals. Articulating and communicating these values, including through
technological tools such as those mentioned in Chapter 2, is step one. We
can then consider how we model, incentivize, and reinforce them.

)uild these bridges toward engaged multigenera-
llaborate around organizational goals. Recogniz-
roactively addressing them is key. Research on
at work[95] identifies four organizationally es-
_ ule roots of most challenges:

- choosing where and when to work;
- communicating among team members;
- getting together;
- finding information or learning new things.

Older colleagues' general conception of work as a "place" versus younger employees' perspective of work as something you do, anywhere, anytime, can be challenging for shared responsibilities. Acknowledging the changing nature of business can be reflected in policies and procedures. Thus, "today most tasks do not require synchronous activities, yet many in older generations—including many senior executives—continue to expect synchronous behavior" despite the realities that the nature of work in most sectors of the economy has changed from the 8 to 5 of previous iterations of work life.[96] In addition, communication can be an issue.

> The crux of most technology-based team misunderstandings is not the technology *per se*—it is how team members interpret each others' intentions based on communication approaches. Younger members are accustomed to rapid responses from peers; they are likely to feel frustrated and, at times, rejected if they don't hear from older colleagues for a day or so. Team members from older generations may not only be uncomfortable with digital communication, they may even feel offended by a lack of face-to-face or at least voice-to-voice interaction, or left out of the loop.[97]

Additionally, the nature of scheduling can be a concern, with the flexibility of millennials contrasting with the preference for preplanning by older colleagues. Finally, older professionals may often be linear learners with a desire to absorb requisite information via training and manuals before beginning the task at hand, while millennials are largely "on demand" learners that figure things out along the way, reaching out to personal contacts with relevant expertise as needed, with "[millennials] likely to be bored and turned off by a project that begins with a lengthy training phase . . . [and older workers] annoyed by [millennials'] frequent questions and requests for input".[98]

One additional insight merits consideration. Research indicates very real differences in the perceptions of management and authority at work, with "baby boomers" and older members of "Generation X" coming of age with a distrust of leaders, and believing that the best work is performed without direct supervision.[99] Millennials, conversely, tend to trust authority figures and look to them for guidance, and this difference poses unique challenges for intergenerational effectiveness at work.

> Forty years ago, young boomers were famous for wanting more personal freedom to direct their lives as they wished, without interference from authority figures in families, schools, or workplaces. In today's workplace, these attitudes have been turned upside-down. It is the younger generation of workers—millennials—who most welcome a closer relationship with supervisors. And it is the older generation of workers—those same boomers—who least welcome a closer relationship.[100]

These differences, as we have discussed, can manifest in many ways. But these characteristics can be channeled to positively impact our organizations. Millennials want consistent feedback and redirection so that they can minimize uncertainty and make sure they are on track for successful achievement of these goals. They want to please the boss and do their job the right way the first time.[101]

Many of the potential pitfalls in intergenerational connection can be mitigated with communication and understanding. Clear expectations on the front end of shared tasks must be explicitly determined. Openness to different ways of thinking is invaluable to intergenerational effectiveness, and allows for voicing ideas, questions, and approaches that can enhance the ethical climate of the organization through greater engagement and transparency. Some of the techniques provided in these chapters can help, for example, starting by explicitly naming shared goals and values, in collaboration with colleagues, and with attention to differences in respectful and open ways. The emerging models of flatter organizational structures rather than the purely hierarchical approach, and greater interest in and potential for interaction with aspirational leaders, facilitates this intergenerational collaboration. Millennials can help us build more collaborative and effective workplaces.

An interactive activity corporations and universities around the country have used to illustrate issues of collaboration, innovation, and creativity is the "marshmallow challenge"—using simple materials like uncooked spaghetti, participant teams are challenged to build the tallest freestanding structure supporting the marshmallow. Who typically excels at this challenge? Kids—kindergarteners in particular. They prototype and use hands-on, experiential methods of devising their structure—older participants plan and plan, and then plan some more. Interactive, iterative experiences with feedback loops can be invaluable for problem solving at work. Consider one millennial's reflection on his introduction to using computers: *"Our teacher would say 'go ahead and take a few minutes and try things out on the computer, explore the buttons and start looking things up.'. . . . that curiosity is something that characterizes the way we are today."*[102]

Acknowledging the Benefit of Engaged, Ethical Cultures

Research on corporate best practices for millennial management[103] includes suggestions specific to cultivating teamwork, effective multitasking, and fostering dialogue—all characteristics of millennial workers and the focus of this chapter. These strategies foster an organizational culture of openness, transparency, and shared purpose that promotes opportunities for voicing values and can be foundational for ethical organizations. These include several approaches.

First, attention can be paid to physical space, including lowering walls between workspaces and designing opportunities for connection such as dynamic break rooms. Zappos.com, for example, signals this from the start of each day because workers at every level of the company enter through the same front door, and Zappos provides free lunch to all employees. Second, companies can consider hosting events—off- and on-site—that allow for engagement and connection. When structured around community service opportunities these events can enhance productivity, team capacities, and company engagement while modeling business as community citizen. Third, companies can foster peer interaction through "onboarding" practices that encourage interaction with existing employees, recognition of employees and teams who achieve organizational goals, and enhancing technology to facilitate team connectivity. Some strategies on effectively using technology are provided in Chapter 2. Recognition can be communicated through these tools or in person, including techniques such as direct communication between senior and junior employee when the junior achieves a milestone—given only when it is earned, and as soon as possible after achievement—and, perhaps, communicated to the organization.

Additionally, companies can allow for consistent accessibility and connection with management. Some companies suggest the act of managers walking around the organization and a literal "open door" policy; others create online portals that function as modern-day suggestion boxes. Here we can consider "highly present role models"[104] as an effective mantra. Other suggestions include "leveling" the value of all workers by providing health insurance and stock options to all, modeled perhaps most prominently by Starbucks; rating 401(k) portfolios for sustainability, which can engage younger and more experienced employees and spur productivity; consideration of approaches such as "reverse mentoring," perhaps in the area of technology, where astute millennials can mentor senior executives on technological tools and trends; and recognition of service anniversary awards.

Experts in the field share the perspective that millennials' inclinations and motivations will change the nature of work for the better. "Innovation thrives when information is unfettered, education is nurtured, people can readily form new groups, and decision-making is inclusive," and to compete for the best young talent, companies must change in fundamental ways.[105] In a move reversing years of tradition, Goldman Sachs recently announced a goal to improve working conditions for its junior bankers by reducing their time spent at work (now advising their employees that an average work week is [only?] 70 to 75 hours, when no such guidelines existed before)—a change prompted in part by the loss of talent to start-ups.[106] Other banks have followed, introducing varying policies with such names as "protected weekends." Early feedback suggests that these new policies have measurable positive effect, and that the effect extends to others in the organization. As one analyst from Goldman noted in an article for Businessweek, "All of the new initiatives, such as no work on Saturdays for analysts and associates, have begun to change mindsets . . . Executives, rather than dwelling on the industry's pressures, speak of the need for a well-rounded life."[107]

Thus, even those organizations in highly regulated or time-sensitive industries can benefit from changes that maximize millennial contribution. Transparency in the recruiting process about the required time spent at work or other factors relating to these issues signal respect for the candidate and will allow for a determination of fit early in the process. Considerations of changes within the organization that align with these work preferences may be transformative for all.

Companies are vulnerable if they do not embrace methods to cultivate young talent, characteristics required for competitiveness in this environment, namely "transparency, free flow of information, and inclusiveness that millennials highly value—and that are also essential for learning and successful innovation." Thus, "rather than complaining [about them], it's time to embrace millennials for what they have to offer, to add experience from older workers to the mix, and to watch innovation explode."[108]

I have learned from the examples of my students as they navigate early career challenges, and this penchant for connectedness and transparency has been a net positive. Students have shared stories of internship challenges that involved uncertainty about the ethical questions including billable hours, expense reporting, client communication, and other very real concerns. For just one example, one student interning at a prestigious investment bank had questions about the appropriateness of a recommendation he and his supervisor had been asked to formulate for the board of directors regarding new investment opportunities. The student first collected data that seemed to confirm his concern, vetted his questions with a trusted friend, and then framed his concerns as questions he raised in a respectful, nonconfrontational manner with his supervisor. The act of raising the questions led his supervisor to view the transaction more closely; he was impressed with the intern's diligence and this student received an employment offer from that firm upon graduation. I am optimistic that he, and the firm, will benefit from his commitment to ethical decision making.

These examples are illustrative for other students. These types of "case studies" are invaluable to me as an instructor, and likewise can be helpful for managers with their young employees. In this way, we are modeling and exploring potential interactions between employee and supervisor, identifying the *Giving Voice to Values* techniques, such as those the student in this episode displayed including collecting data to clarify and support his position, acknowledging his role within the organization as an intern who could frame his concerns by asking questions of his more senior colleague, and embracing a tone of shared learning and purpose. Dialogue among employees and with management thus operationalizes some of the key components of the *Giving Voice to Values* approach, including voice, normality, purpose, and self-knowledge and alignment.

"Take Me to Your Leaders"

We also know that millennials are poised to respond to organizational structures and leaders when explicitly introduced to them. Unlike previous generations, such as "Gen Xers" who largely created new paradigms for work including freelancing and other models, "millennials care about authenticity and institutional values because they are counting on working within organizations to drive change. . . . [They] seem much more inclined to operate within existing structures. Thus far, they have been able to rely on institutions to provide them with the resources and support they need to solve the tasks set before them, and they are likely to continue to do so."[109] This sensibility bodes extremely well for our businesses. "The members of this generation have a great deal to bring to the organizations within which they operate. Their comfort with technology enables them to not only access information and resources creatively and easily, but also to think and function in a world that, to them, has always been without boundaries . . . . [T]hey are, as a rule, people- and organization-oriented rather than alienated, thus easing the process of engaging and acculturating them."[110]

We saw this willingness to learn and take queues from leadership throughout our student survey and focus group results. One student shared this anecdote of positive professional development he experienced:

> At [the large firm where I interned last summer] I was the only one within probably twenty or thirty years of my age in my department. . . . Instinctively when I got there I thought if I had questions, even quick ones, I should email my superiors. After a very short period I realized that they preferred, and it was easier, for me to walk a few minutes to their office and ask them face-to-face. I quickly adapted to how they did things and it ended up being better.

Reflecting the sentiments expressed in our own study, a 2013 Millennial Branding study finds that these workers largely express a positive view of their managers, and appreciate the experience, wisdom, and willingness to mentor that their leaders possess.[111] Managers in the 2013 study expressed some concerns about their millennial employees, including that some have unrealistic compensation expectations, a poor work ethic, and are easily distracted. The research team suggests that the number one thing managers must do to engage millennials is to set expectations clearly and consistently, and to clarify the path toward leadership for the younger employee. Millennials want to know their path, and they want to learn why they are doing a task a certain way.

This potential for engagement may again be under-realized in our companies. According to a large national study, only about half of the millennials feel that the organization for which they work encourages employees to suggest new ways of doing things or rewards them for innovative ideas, and only about half of them agree that their organization does all it can to develop leadership potential.[112]

A senior executive in a top professional services firm in our study described the primary management task as managing expectations. Recognizing this tendency to desire open and consistent feedback, along with the penchant for recognition and advancement, successful managers articulate roles, responsibilities, and what it takes to advance clearly often. Formal rotation programs, innovative training, and other proaches signal and institutionalize this commitment. Millennials respond to this clarity and will respect the process if they understand it. It also reflects the open, transparent, and collaborative cultures that characterize the most successful of our businesses.

Ethical Engagement at Work

Research on character development in the context of professional life can be considered in the context of multigenerational work cultures. Character, after all, embodies traits and virtues that with practice become good habits. These traits, virtues, and habits are discovered by witnessing and imitating the behavior of others and must be cultivated deliberately. Further, virtues must be examined within a community setting. Thus, in addition to being within the domain of family, education, and other formative experiences, character development clearly belongs at work.

Considerations of our past and future "selves"—what we wanted to become, who we envisioned ourselves to be, and where we will be 5, 10, 20 years out—is positively associated with ethical behavior. An interesting opportunity might be considering whether cultivating those cognitive and emotional queues as a form of self-assessment can help us develop our own moral courage, and help us connect to one another. Can we see something of ourselves in that young new hire? Can we appreciate the concerns of an experienced worker considering his or her legacy after retirement?

Additionally, as we consider young professionals we must acknowledge their training ground—our business schools. Educators play a critical role in this development, and managers may be able to apply their observations at work. Scholarship around the development of leadership character in business schools suggests that character development is essential to moving beyond only acquisition of functional content to developing the capacity to impact today's business challenges.[113] The best of our business schools are thinking carefully and strategically about their role in cultivating tomorrow's leaders in a context in which the stakes are extremely high. Courses, experiential opportunities, and other activities

e ideas of socially responsible business, environ-
ibility, the intersection between politics, eco-
lative environment, socio-political historical
globe, economic inequity, and other critical
.c absolutely necessary. Equipped with this awareness
..petency in solution seeking, young professionals are poised for
meaningful impact in our organizations and societies.

What can the research tell us about minimizing the potential for
unethical behavior, and how to mitigate this risk? It has been suggested
that narrow approaches to cultivating negotiation skills at work, a critical competency at all levels of business, have resulted in a generation of
leaders who make ethical compromises; by embracing the GVV approach
of self-awareness and alignment, young professionals can create positive impact for themselves and their organizations. We must start with
acknowledging our values, and attempt to align them with our work.
"Business schools and professors need to help students look inward to
see the person they become when they negotiate. The way to do this is
by showing students how to bring to the negotiating process their full
selves from the roles they play in life—account manager, mentor, sibling,
adventure traveler—along with the associated values, strengths, creativity,
and passion."[114] Embracing our whole selves at work is good for all of
us. "The benefits extend beyond the negotiation task. This approach can
transform the conversation from 'I win, you lose' into more collaborative
discussions about how, through combined efforts, people can explore and
create better results for all parties. It also helps people form stronger connections and build better relationships with their negotiating partners,
because there will be a feeling of trust and respect."[115] The role of business
schools is emphasized here as well; by showing students how to be genu-
ine in strategic dialogue at work, we prepare them for true leadership.

Thus, we return again to engagement within the organization. Connections among employees may also reduce moral transgressions. An
engaged organization can be compared to one in which "the lights are
shining"—thus, one provocative study shows that physical darkness can
conceal identity and encourage unethical behavior. It can induce a psychological feeling of illusory anonymity that disinhibits dishonest and

self-interested behavior, regardless of actual anonymity.[116] An extension of this idea suggests that transparency and the lack of feelings of anonymity help "shine a light" and create cultures of mutual responsibility and engagement.

As we consider the issue of "voice," we can reflect on the emerging challenges facing General Motors in the wake of recalls and failures to communicate problems. Perhaps one of the most damning pieces of this convoluted puzzle was release of internal documents with specific instruction around language to be used by employees discussing the problems. A 68-item list of "banned words" not to be used by employees documenting the safety issues is perhaps as direct an example as possible around the notions of voice at work. This explicit attempt to negatively shape voice may be a reflection of the lack of transparency and willingness to confront and manage challenges that are necessary to successfully display ethical leadership.

How else can we mitigate the risk of unethical behavior at work? James Lang's research[117] on cheating behaviors in the academic setting reminds us that when students believe that their professors are caring and invested in their learning, cheating rates are lower. This dynamic extends to the corporation. Millennials are relational—they perform for (and leave) managers and leaders, they do not perform for (or leave) the company—they "quit the boss, not the job." Investing in your talent, and modeling effective behavior, is mutually beneficial. Peer and direct supervisor interaction is key—the "tone in the middle" matters.

From Engaged Connections to Effective Teams

Open and connected cultures set the stage for collaborative employee impact. Experts in talent management acknowledge a need for careful consideration of "teaming" at work. Effective team participation requires the establishment of relationships. These can be enhanced in new and important ways by embracing millennials values, for example, as one of our corporate respondents indicated, *this includes willingness to accept diversity and include nontraditional team members."* These connections must be considered thoughtfully or we run the risk of throwing people together in counter-productive ways. Another corporate executive in our study noted, *"there is a sense of collaboration in that [millennial employees] want to be part of the team immediately. However, they often fail to earn their spot as older colleagues have done. And once on the team, they seek leadership positions before establishing a grasp of the basics."*

Additionally, today's new professionals may define relationships differently than experienced workers. Face-to-face interaction may not be a prerequisite in this era of social media. This fluidity of interaction has implications for how teams function at work. Additionally, there is a challenge to effective team structuring, given millennial penchant for individual achievement. Thus, "while the millennials ultimately value working on teams, there is also a perceived need for independence and being able to control the process to get the job done. . . . [T]his seems to be a misalignment in terms of these values. This generation exhibits a tendency to have the mentality of being able to complete tasks by themselves. . . ."[118] Yet these tendencies need not be a barrier: "[T]he alignment is in the infrastructure provided for the team and then allowing the individuals to work independently within these parameters. Setting the parameters of the work space and enabling them to operate within this space will allow them to utilize their creativity in order to best accomplish the job."[119]

Both new workers and experienced professionals will benefit from clear dialogue around expectations and contributions, and perhaps reimagining notions of teams and leadership. A useful approach to fostering multigenerational collaboration at work involves presenting guidelines for effective engagement. This method of building bridges among the generations involves conversational learning, which starts with shared agreement around putting the organization first. Conversational learning also includes awareness that we all have biases and "blind spots," and acknowledging an open-mindedness to learning from others, a conscious effort to listen, and an agreement that engagements be characterized by self- and other-respect. These specific "ground rules" can be presented to employees in the context of training, development, peer coaching, and other activities.[120]

Many of our best companies are incorporating these techniques of explicitly naming these challenges, bringing them to the forefront, and collaborating around solutions. Our corporate executives cited several examples, including presentations regarding generational differences, gamification of training, diversity councils around generational differences, training videos exploring bridging the differences, and group calls with required attendance at all levels of the organization. One executive we surveyed includes not only project updates and responsibilities in company-wide meetings, but recognition of milestones including positive results for clients, new babies, and other important events—this reinforces connections, and fosters appreciation for the challenges and joys of various life stages.

Connected Contributions to Ethical Cultures at Work

Connected employees provide a foundation for shared efforts toward organizational success in a collaborative, ethical manner. Our task as experienced professionals and leaders is to show new businesspeople that it is in their best interest to be ethical and effective at work. Ethical decision making can allow for alignment between our own values and those of our organization. Bill Gates famously appealed to two major drivers of human behavior—self-interest and caring for others—in his call toward "creative capitalism."[121] He acknowledged that the greatest challenges we face, in business and society, demand big solutions. This dynamic operates within our organizations and reflects the nature of ethical business. Meeting financial goals sustainably can only come with simultaneous consideration of the triple bottom line of business—economic, social, and environmental performance. Organizational goals can reflect pursuit of success across these three realms. Young talent, with their penchant for values-based business, can be a crucial part of the process.

Harnessing and channeling the ambition and big ideas of business toward ethical impact is the province of our managers. But these calls for and examples of responsible leadership must not only come from the top. For effective engagement of young talent, this motivation can also be peer-led. Today's emerging leaders are peer-connected and peer-motivated. A recent book with a fascinating look at the power of these social networks[122] reminds us that recognizing and capitalizing on these dynamics are critical to behavior and outcomes. Our connections with other people influence aspects of our lives as diverse as our health and emotions to our political preferences and economic prosperity, and are only becoming more complex and acute in the age of the internet.[123] These phenomena are only heightened for our networked young professionals.

Levering connections toward collaborative team motivation can be an approach toward maximizing effective, ethical organizations. We know that strategic and integrated CSR is critical for today's companies, and that CSR involves, at its root, connections with and impact on others. New studies indicate the specific ways that organizations actually enhance the employee and customer experience by incorporating CSR, and reflect the role of community building and collaborative engagement of employees in CSR strategies. CSR programs help bridge gaps for employees seeking commonalities with senior management, their boss, and their customers, and contribute to positive changes in the dynamics of these relationships by enhancing employee engagement and customer-service performance.[124] Exciting new research finds that work "meaningfulness" is largely perceived by employees as related to perceptions of how their company treats others—thus, not only do employees care about how they themselves are treated by the organization, but they care *more* deeply whether their organization treats third parties (customers, consumers, communities) well.[125] Millennials are primed for both this connection with management and others, and with values-based motivation.

Thus, discussion of ethical impact provides a shared space where employees and their managers can interact, reflecting a key desire of millennial talent for both engaged and socially conscious work. General Electric chairman and CEO Jeff Immelt has remarked that sustainability topics have been the single most galvanizing issues in the areas of innovation, employee motivation, and engagement that he has seen in his company.[126] The late Ray Anderson, groundbreaking sustainable business pioneer at world-leading commercial and residential carpet company Interface, provided an early and much-replicated model for combining sustainability strategies and profitability that transformed his industry.

The notion of voice matters in this consideration of connection as well—"you can tell your CSR story in a compelling way [by communicating activities with current and future employees online, in employee newsletters, and in recruiting materials], encourage people to get involved and champion folks who are involved by highlighting their efforts."[127] This communication—regular, consistent, aspirational, and specific—can be a powerful tool, and one that resonates well with millennial recruits and employees. The benefits of such communication extend beyond employee stakeholders—both large and small firms reap substantial benefits from sharing information on CSR with consumers, investors, and other stakeholders. Research findings indicate that this type of communication reaps significant long-term financial value, and reflect the "causal conclusion that good CSR performance leads to enhanced financial performance."[128]

A piece on "resolutions for aspiring leaders" concludes with advice for emerging leaders from the millennial generation:

> Ask more questions than you answer. With the high velocity of change in the world, it is impossible to have answers to all the important questions. Much more important is a deep curiosity about the world and the ability to frame the right questions in profound ways. The world's toughest problems cannot be solved by you or any one organization. Your role will be to bring the right people together to address the challenging issues you raise. Our research demonstrates that the biggest mistakes result from decisions made by people without deep consideration of thoughtful questions.[129]

The process of enhancing our ethical commitment is ongoing, for all of us. Millennials entering professional life are in a profound place. "The maturation of human morality will, in many ways, resemble the maturation of an individual person. As we come to understand ourselves better – who we are, and why we are the way we are—we will inevitably change ourselves in the process. Some of our beliefs and values will survive this process of self-discovery and reflection, whereas others will not".[130] Sociologist Christian Smith wrote a wonderful book[131] about emerging adults that calls us to understand and explain young millennials within the broader context of American culture and society. Smith cites changing roles, differences in youth socialization, mass consumerism, interlocked institutions, disconnection between older adults and young people, and American individualism as contextual factors that must be acknowledged. Smith argues that we can all flourish only by recognizing the macro-social dimensions of our challenges, by explicitly considering moral reasoning, encouraging civil, functional debate on our most pressing issues, and by fostering intergenerational connections. Managed well, the workplace can be a critical space for this development.

CSR as Competitive Advantage in Attracting and Retaining Top Talent

Research on employee recruitment indicates that an organization's corporate social performance, or the organization's commitment to principles, policies, and practices relating to social responsibilities and relationships with stakeholders, affects attractiveness as an employer, and this dynamic is expected to become even more significant. Corporate social performance indicators can give organizations an immediate competitive advantage by attracting a larger applicant pool.[132] One study finds that "signal-based mechanisms," or signals job seekers receive about the company's social performance are important; thus, perceptions of the company by the potential employees, including anticipated pride from being affiliated with that organization, their perceived value fit with the organization, and their exceptions about how the organization treats its employees are related to perceptions of the company's prosocial performance.

Google, a perennial favorite on the "most desirable companies to work for" lists, has been lauded for its unconventional hiring and management practices. As Tom Friedman reflects in a much-circulated *New York Times* op-ed, Google attracts so much talent it can afford to look beyond most traditional hiring metrics like GPA and test scores. Rather, they can focus on hiring attributes including technical ability and general cognitive ability, defined not as I.Q., but as "learning ability"—the ability to process on the fly, to pull together disparate bits of information—gleaned by structured behavioral interviews that are validated for predictive qualities. Other attributes they pursue include leadership potential, which is defined to include emergent traits such as stepping up to lead and step-ping aside to allow someone else to lead, and humility and ownership, including intellectual humility that allows for learning and embracing ideas of others. As Friedman notes, "The world only cares about—and pays off on—what you can do with what you know. . . . And in an age when innovation is increasingly a group endeavor, it also cares about a lot of soft skills—leadership, humility, collaboration, adaptability and lov-ing to learn and re-learn. This will be true no matter where you go to work."[133] And while Google may be an outlier in its hiring practices, it may also be predictive—its ability to attract top young talent may afford it this approach, yet it may also be because of it—a lesson other companies may adapt for their own organizations.

Ethical Cultures in Multigenerational Workplaces

A comprehensive and helpful study by the Ethics Resource Center (ERC)[134] notes several important implications for ethical cultures in the context of the generations. First, the ERC study notes that a criti-cal indicator of workplace culture is whether employees feel pressure to compromise standards—not surprisingly, the more pressure, the more misconduct—and younger workers are more likely than their older col-leagues to feel pressured by others to break the rules. Their data indicate that the more time spent at work the more the feeling of pressure eases as workers learn ways of coping with their work environment.

In addition, the rates of reporting misconduct are increasing for all age groups—the data show no age-related differences in this key measure of ethical cultures, and because this shift from very different levels in the historic patterns of reporting has occurred only recently, the ERC suggests that this change to more reporting was largely driven by millennials.[135]

Finally, fascinating patterns emerge when considering *to whom* each generation considers reporting misconduct—while more experienced workers consult company resources for help with work-related issues, younger workers consult family and friends.[136] These data have impor-tant implications for managers concerned about ethical conduct (in other words, all managers). The news is optimistic and manageable—millennials also exhibit the greatest sensitivity to ethics and compliance training.[137]

Research on best practices in management reflects approaches in which millennial talent may be uniquely positioned to excel, and acknowledges engagement with multigenerational colleagues as necessary for success. Those studying new managers found that preparing for the realities of leadership includes recognizing that authority is not conferred by title, rather a "web of interdependencies," and that "new managers soon learn that when direct reports are told to do something, they don't necessarily respond. In fact, the more talented the subordinate, the less likely she is to simply follow orders."[138] Further, "[o]ver time, good managers find they must earn their subordinates' respect and trust in order to exercise significant authority. They need to demonstrate to subordinates their own character, their competence, and their ability to get things done before those subordinates are likely to follow their lead."[139]

This can be a challenge for young leaders, and for managers of multigenerational teams. "New managers, insecure in their roles, often seek absolute compliance to orders from their subordinates, particularly in their early days. But what they learn over time is that 'compliance' is not the same as 'commitment.'"[140] This results in challenges at multiple levels. Without commitment, employees are not motivated to take initiative, and if subordinates are not taking initiative, the manager can not effectively delegate. "The challenge for managers is to nurture a strong sense of common commitment to shared goals—rather than one of blind allegiance to the managers' dictates.[141] The American Management Association notes that one of the key leadership behaviors that gets in the way of effectiveness and innovation is a leader's inability to listen well; this tendency affects the culture of open collaboration, and inhibits informal dialogue required for creative and critical problem solving.[142] Other potential pitfalls include framing constructive challenging of others to think critically as overt criticism, and leaders taking ownership of an idea put forward by employees, which results in feelings of disengagement and lack of motivation. A final challenge is failing to align creative thinking directly with elements of success as articulated by the vision and strategy of organization: leaders often fail to focus sufficiently on communicating these key elements of success.[143] All of these tasks can be addressed through cultivating true connections, and emphasizing alignment of activities and goals.

Shared goals are key and through collaboration they can be nurtured. Interconnectedness may come naturally to young talent; cultivating and appreciating these connections are a distinguishing and important characteristic of millennials. Thus, due to their upbringing, "millennials can heed moral exemplars, and respond to principled leaders, far better than most of today's adults could when young."[144] These leaders can normalize ethical considerations at work, and provide models for voicing values.

Millennials have good reason to be mindful of the pressures around ethical challenges. The structural advantages that can sometimes be in place for senior-level management may not be accessible to young professionals, and when ethically questionable behavior occurs, there is the potential for scapegoating. Consider the case of Betty Vinson. Vinson, an accountant at WorldCom, ended up in jail for her role in the accounting scandal that weighed in at $11 billion. Cynthia Rowley ended up on the cover of Time magazine as a "woman of the year" for her role in blowing the whistle. Of course these two women were responsible for their choices in the face of pressure to perform inconsistently with their values. How and why they chose to act, or not act, in the face of this pressure is a perfect teaching case (and is available from the Harvard Business School Case Collection[145]). However, case after case illustrates the vulnerability of young talent. Senior leaders often leverage protections that are unavailable to young employees. Careful decision making early in our careers is imperative.

The ERC also provides tips for engaging millennials around ethics at work. These data do not suggest that organizations must revamp their ethics programs for each generation; rather, communication about available resources for ethics at work, and the organization's commitment to ethical leadership, can be emphasized in different ways. These approaches for millennials include techniques such as communicating the company's commitment to ethics in terms of people and relationships guided by integrity, focusing on messaging from colleagues and immediate supervisors who are local and influential to this young talent, emphasizing the ethics and compliance program as opportunities to interact with knowledgeable colleagues who can provide support and guidance, building opportunities for discussion and interaction into ethics and compliance training, providing ways for millennials to share input into organizational standards and systems, and communicating that when employees do report misconduct it is an interactive process.[146]

Encouragingly, despite media coverage that may suggest otherwise, workplace misconduct has actually declined steadily and significantly in the last decade and is now at an all-time low.[147] Researchers in the ERC study ascribe this decline in part to economic instability and its relationship with workers' confidence and penchant for risk-taking. I contend the influx of young talent who studied business in the post-Enron era with heightened attention to ethics in the classroom, and some of the other characteristics of this generation may also be a factor.

Evidence clearly suggests that "increasingly sophisticated ethics and compliance programs are creating new norms in worker conduct. By almost every measure, companies are working harder to build strong cultures and further develop their ethics and compliance programs."[148] Some highlights of this data include the increase in companies providing ethics training rising from 74 to 81 percent in the past three years, an increase in companies including ethical conduct as a performance measure in employee evaluations, and almost 75 percent of companies communicating internally about disciplinary actions when wrongdoing occurs.[149] Millennials and their managers are helping to drive this trend with an attitude of ethical business as a natural extension of the business functions, and an enhanced focus on transparency and communication.

Again, connectedness is key. Fascinating research on the "cheater's high," or positive affect in individuals triggered by unethical behaviors, may be one more challenge to ethics at work—yet an important caveat to the research suggesting individuals who engage in unethical actions feel satisfaction is actually mitigated by "social consensus regarding the ethicality of the act" and that individuals are less likely to engage in unethical behavior if they perceive their action as having no obvious victim.[150] Our technologically driven culture may make this concern even more acute. The internet can create more distance between us and our actions.

It's created a distance between us and the people who would suffer the consequences. If you're dealing mortgage-backed securities, think about how many steps there are between you and the consequences of your action, and how easy it is, [to create an] anonymous general group that all of a sudden you can misbehave toward.[151]

This research suggests that incentives along with cultural norms and rewards associated with ethical behavior matter, and that *proximity to those impacted by unethical decisions, along with discussion of stakeholders and the impact of decision-making, reduces the likelihood of engaging in them*—both key findings for organizational cultures intent on engaged and connected employees.

Finally, research and anecdotal advice for managing millennials suggest that loyalty is personal rather than to corporation, so supervisor and other connections are critical—intentionally creating connections between employees produces generous returns and is well worth the effort to design and implement them. These relationships can assist in institutionalized mentoring, or help foster organic mentor-like connections—both leader-led and peer-to-peer mentoring. We will discuss this millennial characteristic next.

Chapter 3: Action Items

Engaged, connected, and values-driven workplaces are primed to flourish. Following are chapter highlights that managers and millennials can consider to foster effective, ethical multigenerational workplaces.

(1) *Acknowledge that engaged employees and collaborative workplaces matter now more than ever.* Create connections between employee and supervisor, and among colleagues, which are expressed desires of millennials and can foster effective organizations for all.

(2) *Foster engaged and connected cultures that make for productive and successful companies.* Creating opportunities for connectedness can include peer recognition of goal achievement, acknowledging individual and team milestones across all levels of the organization, and modeling accessible and engaged management.

(3) *Focus on shared values* by articulating the mission of the organization clearly and often. Incorporate off- and on-site events that allow for engagement and connection, including those around social impact issues such as community service that can enhance team building and commitment.

(4) *Acknowledge that millennials, perhaps more than any other generation in the workplace, respond to and appreciate training and development.* Due to their formative experiences and connections with parents and other authority figures, millennials are poised to receive professional development at work when clearly connected with impact and meaning.

(5) *Acknowledge possible differences explicitly and collaboratively* through discussion of generational differences, presenting guidelines for effective engagement and reinforcing respectful dialogue.

(6) *Integrate CSR topics throughout the organization as a means of engendering engaged and productive employees.* Acknowledge that millennials can help drive these strategies, with their networking and awareness strengths as assets. Consider approaches such as dialogue and exercises around self-assessment and alignment with organizational values.

CHAPTER 4

Mentor Me, Please!

All photographs used with permission, Copyright © 2014 by Della Dewald

Though a common refrain seems to be that millennials prefer to go rogue and abandon notions of acting as "company men (and women)," research indicates, and anecdotal evidence supports, that millennials actually display strong preference for connections, mentoring, and relationships at work. They are comfortable with and used to engaging with parents, teachers, coaches, and others around their personal and professional development in ways that are unprecedented. They may even view their supervisors as "workplace parents"[152] with the related desire to please (and, perhaps uncomfortably for some managers, transcend traditional boundaries of employer–employee).

This proclivity for connection with experienced workers suggests opportunities for managers to develop young leaders toward shared goals. It also has implications for integrating discussions of ethical decision making firmly within the organization. Scholars identify key characteristics of high-performing CEOs to include both skills in integrating multiple disciplines into systemic approaches to building better-performing organizations, and explicit integration of personal values and principles into their leadership.[153] This is clear evidence of the role of identifying purpose, broadly and thoughtfully defined, as a critical skill for business leaders. Further, leaders have an invaluable role in building institutions that do both well (financially) and good (prosocial contribution). This is aligned exactly with the *Giving Voice to Values* (GVV) approach of learning from successful examples of those who have acted on their values, and identifying the practical steps necessary for doing so ourselves. Values discussions are brought to the table, normalized, and successful resolution of challenges is modeled. These "high-ambition" leaders, those who define purpose to include creating economic and societal value, represent the GVV model of leadership development. Engaging with young professionals, modeling effective behavior, and fostering organizational culture that rewards values-based decision making benefit the young employee, the managers, the organization, and its stakeholders.

Modeling and Mentoring through Purpose

Mentoring around ethical leadership for young employees can begin with explicit consideration of purpose, and with engaged leadership that models integration of values at work. We will explore purpose at work more directly in Chapter 5, but acknowledging purpose as a platform for engagement is critical to meaningful mentorship. Consider the example of the medical device company Medtronic, which has turned this consideration of the firm's purpose into its galvanizing message to employees and other stakeholders. The philosophy under cofounder Earl Bakken's leadership was that the company was "not putting a pacemaker into someone's body; we were restoring them to full life and health." They reflected that philosophy by incorporating patient testimony about how their devices changed their lives into trainings and other company milestones so that all employees could reflect on this notion of purpose.[154] Gallup data indicate that only 25 percent of employees feel connection to their company's mission—at Medtronic, 84 percent of their employees feel this alignment.[155] Integrating this sense of compelling purpose throughout the organization aids in promoting a cohesive culture and enhanced commitment by all stakeholders. It provides a rallying point around which new and experienced workers can connect.

Former Medtronic CEO and Harvard professor Bill George suggests that engagement must be driven by leaders who inspire, with managers who:

> work alongside their employees, doing more than their fair share of the most challenging aspects of the work. Their leadership role is to champion the company's mission and values, and to challenge others to meet higher standards on behalf of their customers. . . . The most senior executives . . . should be engaged every day with the first-line [employees who] will be more engaged and productive, . . . and executives will make better informed, more thoughtful decisions about the business because they are so much closer to their markets and the people doing the work.[156]

Modeling effective leadership can be a form of mentoring; opportunities for deliberate modeling and reflection can benefit the leader and the young employee simultaneously. High-performing CEOs are open to learning through feedback and reflection. We know that business students often indicate a struggle to reconcile the messages they receive from parents, peers, supervisors, and their business education—a prosocial conception of business and of business practitioners—with the seemingly endless scandals and purely profit-driven, rather than purpose-driven, businesses. Engagement between our business schools, the training ground for young professionals, and our corporations is essential. The best of our business schools create opportunities for experienced business leaders to become intimately involved with business education through leadership development activities. Speaker series, project-based internships and other curricular experiences, and hands-on case-study approaches in collaboration with business executives are several key approaches.

Encouraging reflection and open communication on building better businesses, together with leaders and with peers, reflects a critical GVV pillar of self-awareness and alignment. Knowing what we value, and considering our values in the context of those shared with leaders we respect, and with our organizations, can be powerful prompts to ethical action. This action orientation is clearly aligned with millennials' goals for impact and engagement. Expressing our intentions, practicing our processes and strategies in front of peers and with aspirational and exemplary role models, and collaborative action resonate with millennials' penchant for collective activity and team response to professional challenges. Our companies can, of course, continue to promote and engage around those who have successfully integrated values and professional life in our businesses through leadership activities and other professional development initiatives. This is mentorship in a broad, and critical, sense.

Linda Treviño and her colleagues suggest a dual-pillar approach to corporate leadership that has implications for modeling and mentoring—it is not enough to "be" a moral manager—our people must know that we are.[157] Being ethical and making good decisions is not enough. Managers must develop a reputation for ethical leadership that includes employee perceptions of the leader as both a moral person and a moral manager. Role modeling, communicating regularly about values, incentivizing and rewarding ethical behavior, and holding people accountable are critical.[158] The role of senior managers in cultivating corporate culture, identifying priorities, and fostering a culture of contribution cannot be overstated: "Leaders can form relationships of trust with followers, empower them through inclusion in decision making, encourage follower growth and success, behave ethically, balance work with vision, and create value—and encourage followers to create value—for others outside of the organization."[159]

The context is also important. The economic environment experienced today may actually bring out the best in our young professionals. Some characteristics of millennials work in their favor, and to the benefit of their employers, during challenging economic conditions. "Management experts note that, while money is important, millennials do not see money as their only source of happiness. Like Generation X workers, they feel rewarded by work arrangements that offer more flexibility and new technology . . . [and] expect to become involved in projects that have a major impact on the organization, soon after their organizational entry."[160] Work structures that enhance efficiencies are aligned well with millennial proclivities. Loyalty at work is to the idea, to the mission, to the purpose—it is personal, not to the corporation—so supervisor and colleague connections are critical and can only be fostered through intentional effort on the part of management. Coaching and collaboration are key. Acknowledging these dynamics may allow managers to encourage these connections in their own organizations, and can assist with meaningful contribution by millennials.

Approaches to Mentoring: Peers, Interaction, and Reflection

In addition to direct and aspirational modeling, other development techniques can be effective with young professionals. One of several tactics is group mentoring. Scholars found that manager-led or peer-to-peer mentoring at top companies, including such approaches as online platforms, leads to decreased training costs and enhanced communication.[161] This approach goes beyond managing millennials—"improving your company's ability to give employees honest, timely, and useful coaching won't benefit just your 20-something workers."[162] In a survey of the importance of managerial skills, participants "in all generations placed a high premium on having a manager who 'will give straight feedback.' And yet when [the researchers] asked 300 heads of HR to rate their managers' competence in the same eight skills, giving feedback was ranked dead last. Clearly, that's a critical gap companies need to bridge."[163]

Further, when researchers interviewed 125 leaders to explore development of alignment around mission and values, and empowering leaders at all levels of the organization, findings indicated that self-awareness is a precursor to emotional intelligence, a critical leadership component. Self-awareness requires real-world, practical experiences, reflection and processing one's experiences, and group interactions that allow sharing experiences and receiving feedback.[164] Lack of attention here is a "missing link" in leadership that has been shown to enhance productivity, and can be cultivated with self-assessment, alignment, and peer coaching—all techniques that can be incorporated into professional training and development.

When managers engage millennials with interactive feedback, voice is acknowledged and developed. These connections can be readily extended to include dialogue on values. Engaging with peers and leaders around our values and our commitment—expressing out loud who we are and who want to be—is key. Through exploration of our self-assessments and alignment with personal and organizational goals, we can all formulate effective, actionable voice. This enhanced self-efficacy leads to improved motivation and job performance.

In one study, those employers who built reflection opportunities into training and development saw work performance that was significantly better than those who did not[165]—a finding supporting an approach that has been underutilized, as expressed by Harvard researcher Francesca Gino: "I don't see a lot of organizations that actually encourage employees to reflect—or give them time to do it. . . . When we fall behind even though we're working hard, our response is often just to work harder. But in terms of working smarter, our research suggests that we should take time for reflection."[166] Incorporating elements of reflection at work—conscious consideration of our actions—is known to enhance job performance.[167] Reflecting on what we have done helps us to be more effective the next time—our self-efficacy increases and we are more motivated to perform better next time. These Harvard researchers suggest that organizations build time for reflection into the work experience in order to "work smarter." These experiences can be structured as team-building professional development opportunities around shared organizational values. This is modeling effective leadership for young talent, and aligns well with their motivations.

Approaches to Mentoring: Broadly Defined

We must also be explicit about what we mean by "mentoring." Weekly fireside chats or play-by-play advising are by no means necessary, and, of course, have productivity problems by definition. If we expand the notion of mentoring to include such aspects as peer-to-peer coaching, leader-led team development sessions, engaging with aspirational role models, clear communication of expectations to all employees, and explicit yet accessible mechanisms for clear and consistent feedback, we are now acknowledging a framework that is both manageable and effective. Coaching by employers need not be overly formal or time consuming—it can be as easy as a quick e-mail response, a text, or a two-minute conversation.[168] Experienced workers benefit as do new hires. Relationships are strengthened and the organization as a whole is more successful.

Another approach has been called "shadowing"—new employees do not simply talk with experienced professionals in the company, they watch these professionals in action. This shadowing can occur at multiple levels—shadowing the owner in customer meetings, the chief engineer for internal processes, and the administrative assistant for the day-to-day dynamics—and involves enough time with them to be able to appreciate the complexities of each task and role. It is to literally walk in the others' shoes, and allows for more thorough understanding of the bigger picture of successful operations.[169]

Additionally, "physical proximity between leaders and employees is not always feasible. But mental or emotional proximity is essential"—an approach called conversational leadership, which we explored briefly in Chapter 3. This approach rejects the "command and control" approach to management—an approach that appears to be ineffective with millennial talent, and is increasingly becoming obsolete. "Globalization, new technologies, and changes in how companies create value and interact with customers have sharply reduced the efficacy of a purely directive, top-down model of leadership."[170] What approaches will replace that model? "Part of the answer lies in how leaders manage communication within their organizations—that is, how they handle the flow of information to, from, and among their employees. Traditional corporate communication must give way to a process that is more dynamic and more sophisticated. Most important, that process must be *conversational*."[171]

Top-down, one-way communication has become unrealistic and inefficient—for example, as discussed in Chapter 2, with the advent of social media, employees have a public voice and leadership must adjust accordingly—and managers can leverage this new reality toward positive organizational development. Economic changes that preference knowledge work over other kinds of labor that require more sophisticated communication, organizational change that reflects flatter and less hierarchical

structures that involve lateral and bottom-up communication, globalization that requires fluid and complex interactions, the influx of young talent
with a preference for dynamic, two-way communication with peers and
their superiors, and technological changes that render static communication obsolete mean that the nature of interaction at work must change.[172]

Scholars have identified elements of organizational conversation
that are critical for navigating this new paradigm, including *intimacy*,
or leaders emphasizing listening to employees rather than speaking to
them, and bottom-up exchanges of ideas with employees; *interactivity*, or
leaders using social and other media tools to facilitate two-way communication, and employees interacting with colleagues on such tools as blogs
and discussion forums; *inclusion*, or leaders involving employees in communicating the company's story, and in acting as brand ambassadors and
thought leaders; and *intentionality*, or leaders building messaging around
corporate strategy and employees taking part in creating this strategy.[173]

How much mentoring is enough? Only three percent of the young
people we surveyed expressed that interaction with their mentors monthly
or less frequently is satisfactory, with 70 percent saying weekly or two to
three times per month is ideal. When it comes to meeting with direct
supervisors, our respondents prefer even more frequent connection, with
82 percent desiring connection at least two to three times per month and
31 percent hoping for weekly connections.

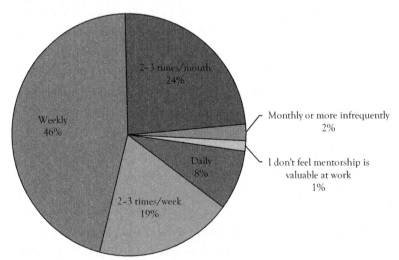

Figure 4.1 *If you feel mentorship is valuable at work, how much*
interaction would you consider ideal? (n=138)

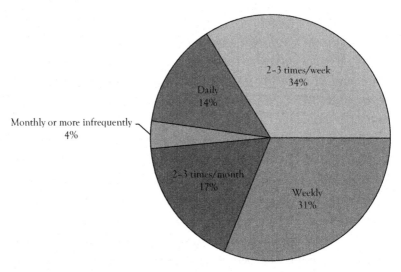

Figure 4.2 How often would you prefer to meet face-to-face with your direct supervisor? (n=138)

Millennials themselves have an important role in this exchange between mentor and mentee. Mentoring is a two-way engagement. One of our corporate managers indicated a concern echoed by several in our study: *"Gen Y is definitely focused on identifying mentors. However, I question their ability to listen and learn. They seem to view mentors more as "contacts" for networking rather than "teachers.""* Young employees, who another manager described as being "like sponges, absorbing everything," will do well to acknowledge experience and organizational wisdom as they navigate these relationships at work. The willingness to learn and grow is often there. As one of our student respondents noted, *"Mentors are the most valuable means of education I have ever had."*

Cultivating Performance through Mentoring

Our corporate respondents reflected several best practice examples for mentoring millennials. Specific approaches include reverse mentoring, for example, regarding technology, such as instances in which young employees provide advice and suggestions around effective use of social media and other tools. Other tips include incorporating professional development programs for new hires focusing on professional expectations in a large organization, coaching and direct involvement when problems occur, and reinforcing successful solutions. One executive noted, *"We have discovered that partnering the millennials with a more experienced worker really helps both of them. The millennials have [technological] skills that often make them much more efficient on the same projects, and the experienced employees have so much valuable experience that it makes for really great teamwork."* These findings echo existing research on managing and mentoring young talent.

These relationships, perhaps around functional activities, can provide a foundation for connections around values and mission that can expand the impact of engaged employees even further. As we consider what works in training and performance management, we can consider another change of frame that aligns with millennial characteristics and can serve to create a more vibrant, transparent, and aspirational culture for all employees. The shift is from performance appraisal—typically annual, often transactional, and backward-looking—to performance development and coaching, which is characterized as relational, amenable to fostering dialogue, involving continuous assessment and recognition, and forward-looking.[174] As another scholar describes, many organizations confuse the term "assessment" with "evaluation." Assessment involves determining effectiveness and/or efficiency of a new plan or policy, or learning about processes. Evaluation, on the other hand, is involved with results and outcomes. While both measure performance, one should focus on process and the other on the bottom line.[175]

Both are critical for millennial development. A more integrated and ongoing performance development process can ensure measurable outcomes and lead to explicit attention to meaning and impact at work. Techniques for evaluation and development abound; so-called 360° evaluations for development, integration with mentoring and peer coaching activities, and innovative training and education programs are just some examples.

Acknowledging, coaching, and celebrating performance should be part of the process to reinforce norms, expectations, and values. These interactions become another opportunity to cultivate organizational values through engagement with employees. It also creates space for employees to voice ideas and opportunities, and for employee concerns to be explored and addressed consistently and thoughtfully, perhaps reducing the need for external approaches (for example, negative "work narration," or even whistleblowing). It can create new opportunities for collecting data to allow for assessment of learning and retention. It is no coincidence that mentoring, training, and development programs are featured prominently in recruiting materials for young talent. Some of our top companies are engaged in exciting examples; we will include reference to some in Chapter 7. We can also consider, for illustration, a suggestion from one of our millennial students in a class dedicated to effective engagement of young talent toward ethical impact at work:

From the start of the development process new hires should receive heavy training and emphasis on ethics and personal responsibility. This training should focus on putting new employees in realistic, industry specific situations that have been experienced by other employees at the firm. Additionally, the training should focus on curbing individual practices that can potentially harm the firm, such as overconfidence, complacency, and self-preservation in train employees with team-oriented solutions to unethical situations and habits. An ethics committee or HR team within the company could carry out this component. The committee should be comprised of members of all ages and departments within the organization in order to both give all company workers a comfortable outlet to contact, to handle ethical situations in different aspects of the business, and to send a message to the rest of the company that this commitment to ethical practices reaches all corners of the organization (MM student).[a]

Given consistent research findings supporting the returns associated with a more thoughtful and integrated performance review and development process, it is surprising that more companies do not invest time and resources into strategic approaches. With millennial talent, direct and

---

[a]These excerpts are derived from papers submitted to this professor in 2013 and 2014 in the senior-level undergraduate course *BAET 30400: Managing and Millennials*, University of Notre Dame. These excerpts will be cited in the book as "*Managing and Millennials* course projects, student perspectives: MM student." Permission for citing assignment excerpts was provided by each student.

consistent feedback seems to be most effective. One scholar studying millennials in business suggests:

> When appraising their work, be direct—millennials tend to put a rosy glow on gently stated complaints. Managers should avoid the "sandwich approach" to feedback, where a criticism is preceded and followed by a positive statement. . . . [I]f managers hedge their criticism with a string of compliments, millennials will tune out the reprimands and "just hear, 'Blah, blah, I'm great.'"[176]

This penchant for directness was echoed in our own focus group of millennial talent, with remarks such as,

"I like when people are honest and very frank with me and if I don't have a direct, objectifiable role to achieve, I'll tend to be less motivated to do things. And if I have [a supervisor] who doesn't tell me exactly what I'm doing wrong or what they actually look for, then that's very frustrating."

Another student suggested this strategy for a proposed evaluation component:

Every quarter, employees would have the option of sitting down with their immediate supervisor to discuss their insights and voice any concerns they may have regarding misalignment between their purpose and their role within the organization. While these meetings are optional every quarter, employees must participate at least once a year. With employees articulating their goals through open discussion, companies will better be able to meet employee needs and keep motivation and satisfaction high (MM student).

We can consider an additional suggestion:

Once a year, each associate would be paired up with a senior manager to discuss their perspectives on their careers. Every pair has to submit something [to the organization] they learned about their partner's generation and why that makes them an asset to the company. There would then be a company-wide conference where the most noteworthy stories are shared with the entire organization. Not only would personal relationships be formed, stereotypes will be proved wrong in the process (MM student).

We can also consider a suggestion that further supports the idea of traditional and reverse mentoring:

[Companies could launch a] mentor/reverse mentor program [which] pairs baby boomers with millennial employees, and encourages both sides to learn from each other. The program requires participants to hold both formal and informal meetings regularly. In formal meetings, two participants talk about their current projects (in confidence), and seek opinions and ideas from the each other. Baby boomers could offer advice based on their extensive working experience, and millennials may provide insights about technology and creative marketing strategies. In informal meetings, participants could have lunch together and share their own personal lives. Such communication creates opportunities for different generations to comprehend and appreciate each other's background, and hence understand how that difference has shaped individuals as how they are now (MM student).

Reinforcing the role of social media as a tool for this cross-generational engagement as we discussed in Chapter 2, we can consider a final suggestion for this engagement:

Companies could have younger, more social media literate employees administering the recruiting Twitter and LinkedIn accounts, while simultaneously having the younger employees aid in improving the technological literacy of some of the more experienced workers. This will not only improve dialogue and connections between older and younger employees hailing from different generations, but will also increase the company's technological capabilities, and develop a trendy and relevant social media presence (MM student).

These suggestions may represent new approaches for managers. Yet we know that young talent is interested in performing well and meeting expectations. They appreciate an optimistic and engaging approach to their development. Who among us does not?

We explore best practices in Chapter 7 but two examples related to mentoring are illustrative here. Citibank offers a "reverse mentoring" program in collaboration with the University of Miami Business School to facilitate interactions between undergraduate and MBA students and Citibank professionals for project-based work around digital technologies, communications, and social media for development of long-term strategies. This approach to harnessing the skills of young talent and leveraging connections between emerging and established business professionals allows millennials the opportunity to share their insights and learn alongside aspirational leaders.

PepsiCo's Connect mentoring program connects young professionals within the company for peer-to-peer networking and exposure of ideas to executives for implementation and sponsorship, supporting recruiting events for new talent, assisting with product development and marketing, and improving work–life balance for all employees—which contributes to the organization, provides management with information on new trends and technologies, and accelerates participants' careers through tangible skill development.

Troubleshooting

What about when things are not so rosy? How might we handle challenges to expectations of the manager and the corporation? How can managers effectively address an implied or explicit questioning of corporate norms and policies? Millennials have been encouraged to take a seat at the table in decision making at home and at school. It is no wonder these tendencies continue at work. An effective approach might be to appeal to their peer and community orientation. Thus, managers can model (or state outright) that certain processes, decisions, and choices were developed and agreed to by the community in which they are operating—rules have come by consensus—and that success in the community depends on respecting them. The issue can be reframed. Managers can foster consideration of proactive, positive change. Thus, if the system or process is not to your liking, rather than noncompliance or avoidance, how can you think about effectively engaging others around enhancing the system or process? Can you work for change within the community's understanding of roles and processes?

Chapter 4: Action Items

Mentoring, broadly defined to include modeling, peer- and leader-led professional development, can channel engaged employees into those that contribute and flourish. Millennials are poised to appreciate and grow within this approach. Below are several tips to consider.

(1) *Through interaction and engagement, managers and other corporate leaders can model values-based decision making toward success for employees throughout the organization.* Modeling and mentoring around purpose can be a powerful galvanizing force for cohesive, productive cultures.

(2) *Managers can encourage reflection and values alignment explicitly through training and development opportunities.* Consider both leader-led and group mentoring, engaging with aspirational role models, and clear feedback loops. Physical proximity may not always be required or possible; mechanisms can include technological approaches such as blogs and discussion boards and face-to-face opportunities incorporating values exercises in training and development.

(3) *Millennials and their more experienced colleagues can be encouraged to be active participants in these exchanges.* Young talent can acknowledge experience and organizational wisdom as essential to workplace success, and experienced workers can signal willingness to collaborate and perform together.

(4) *Reverse mentoring, a shift from performance appraisal to performance management, and other changes to traditional approaches can be successful for all employees in multigenerational cultures.* Acknowledging, coaching, and celebrating performance should be part of the process to reinforce expectations, norms, and values. These occasions become additional opportunities for engagement.

CHAPTER 5

Must Be Meaningful

For both millennials and their managers, intrinsic motivation—or motivation for behavior that comes from within, driven by feelings of inherent satisfaction, joy, the pleasure of learning, and accomplishment—is essential for long-term productivity and development in professional life. Traditional motivation at work has been associated primarily with extrinsic rewards, or those externally motivated factors such as financial rewards (i.e., compensation, bonuses, and so on) and avoiding negative consequences. Of course this matters. Yet research tells us that in the modern workplace, which requires experimentation, creativity, problem solving, and innovation, managers must cultivate intrinsic motivation to maximize performance.[177] Thus, alignment with purpose is key. This consideration of motivation is particularly important for millennials, who reflect these desires for meaning and purpose explicitly, and who directly manifest the changing nature of work.

Thus, not only are financial incentives less effective in motivating performance for creative work, they can actually hinder performance. Scientists have explored the distinction between "algorithmic" tasks, or those in which we follow established instructions down a single path toward one conclusion, and "heuristic" tasks that require experimentation and innovative solutions.[178] Examples of algorithmic work include that of grocery checkout clerks or assembly line workers. Heuristic tasks would be those such as creating an advertising campaign.

We can consider trends in work over time, and implications for today's businesses.

Thus, "during the twentieth century, most work was algorithmic— and not just jobs where you turned the same screw the same way all day long. Even when we traded blue collars for white, the tasks we carried out were often routine. That is, we could reduce much of what we did—in accounting, law, computer programming, and other fields—to a script, a spec sheet, a formula, or a series of steps that produced a right answer."[179] However, workplaces are changing: "The consulting firm McKinsey & Co. estimates that in the United States, only 30 percent of job growth now comes from algorithmic work, while 70 percent comes from heuristic work. A key reason: Routine work can be outsourced or automated; artistic, empathic, nonroutine work generally cannot."[180]

This research has tremendous implications for motivation at work. Harvard Business School researchers have found that the "carrots and sticks" of external rewards and punishments work well for algorithmic tasks, but can be devastating for heuristic work. "Those sorts of challenges—solving novel problems or creating something the world didn't know it was missing—depend heavily on . . . the intrinsic motivation principle of creativity, which holds, in part: 'Intrinsic motivation is conducive to creativity; controlling extrinsic motivation is detrimental to creativity.'"[181] The central thesis of external "carrot and stick" motivation "may actually *impair* performance of the heuristic, right-brain work on which modern economies depend."[182]

Purpose at Work: for Millennials and for All

Because of their capacities and life experiences (i.e., motivation by feelings of esteem and self-worth) millennials are well positioned to champion this revised approach to motivation. Managers can design and incentive training and development activities that recognize this new reality. Of course, the expressed desire of young talent for intrinsic motivation may lead to members of older generations to shake their heads: as one of our corporate respondents noted, *"Being naive and ideological runs amok with this generation. They only want to do work they find meaningful—what the heck does that mean? So, who does the other jobs?"* A new approach, however, does not mean millennials are not capable of or willing to do work that is repetitious, taxing, or otherwise less-than-enchanting.

Rather, the solution seems to be *engagement* around whatever work is being done, and connections with the "big picture" of mission and goals. Affirming that all tasks are vital to organizational functioning and success is key, and explicitly communicating the "why" behind the "what" of our tasks at work resonates particularly with this group. This is not the exclusive province of work with clearly visible connections to "meaning." All of us can create organizations that matter, and all can contribute in ways, large and small, to the purpose of this work. These types of disconnects between the expressed desires of millennials, and the goals and perceptions of their managers, are the areas where engaged communication around values and purpose are so important. Some of the tools of the *Giving Voice to Values* approach, such as those related to reflection and alignment, can help bridge these gaps by helping us define purpose explicitly and broadly, and by doing so together with colleagues.

Purpose at Work: Organizational Effectiveness

This notion of purpose beyond extrinsic motivation extends to the organization. The 2014 Deloitte Core Beliefs & Culture survey reveals that organizations with a strong sense of purpose, defined as a focus on making a positive impact on customers, employees, and society at large, are more confident in growth prospects, are more likely to invest in initiatives associated with long-term growth, and enjoy higher levels of confidence among key stakeholders. Eighty-two percent (82 percent) of over 1,000 respondent executives and employees who work full time for an organization with a strong sense of purpose reflect this confidence in their organization's growth, compared to 48 percent of those who do not.

Similar gaps were found in levels of confidence with respect to increasing investments in new technologies, developing new products and services, and expanding into new markets. "Lack of business confidence has been a hindrance to economic recovery," says Punit Renjen, chairman, Deloitte LLP. "Through our surveys this year and last, evidence is mounting that focusing on *purpose* rather than *profits* is what builds business confidence. This is a critical finding, and underscores the significant impact a 'culture of purpose' can play in fostering a thriving business community."[183]

Consider the example of 3M Corporation, profiled in a Harvard Business Review blog post.[184] Their research and development approach encompasses the "15% rule," which operationalizes elements of reflection and intrinsic motivation into an innovative business strategy. Board chairman William McKnight, who rose from his initial bookkeeping position to leadership, explains the logic of this approach: "Encourage experimental doodling. If you put fences around people, you get sheep. Give people the room they need." Company engineers and scientists can spend up to 15 percent of their time pursuing self-selected projects, able to explore unexpected opportunities for innovations and new approaches. "For example, some employees in the infection-prevention division used their '15% time' to pursue wirelessly connected electronic stethoscopes. The result: In 2012, 3M introduced the first electronic stethoscope with Bluetooth technology that allows doctors to listen to patients' heart and lung sounds as they go on rounds, seamlessly transferring the data to software programs for deeper analysis."[185] Young professionals are wired to flourish in these new professional spaces.

Business purpose as solely profit-motivated has been soundly rejected by the majority of millennials. A 2014 survey of employees at a top professional services firm revealed that almost 90 percent of millennials believe that business is a critical part of the solution to unemployment and nearly 75 percent say the same about income and wealth inequalities.[186] Other findings illustrate even broader vision for the potential of business, with more than 80 percent believing that business has the potential to address the other two top-rated societal challenges identified by respondents—climate change/environmental protection and resource scarcity. More than half of millennials feel that business can develop services and products or incorporate behaviors that can have a positive impact on each of the 20 challenges included in the survey.[187]

In my own classes, we talk about the role of business in wealth creation, and the acknowledgment that wealth in society includes much more than financial metrics like GDP. Wealth, broadly defined, must include physical (natural and produced), financial, human, and social capital.[188] Defining wealth broadly opens the door for considerations of the purpose and nature of business, and the role of a variety of stakeholders in business decision making. Students in our survey reflect this sentiment in their aspirations for their work life.

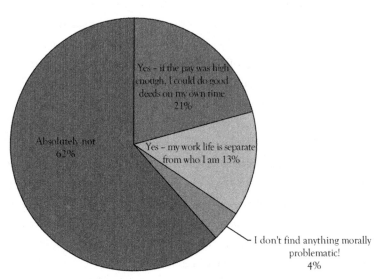

Figure 5.1 Could you work for a company that offers a product or service you personally find morally problematic? (n = 138)

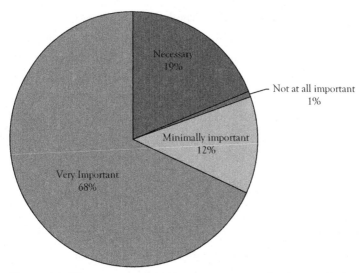

Figure 5.2 How important is aligning your personal values with the values espoused by the company for which you would like to work? (n = 138)

Earlier iterations of the survey of employees at a top professional services firm reflect the same broad notion of the purpose of business that can not simply be explained away as the naiveté of youth: "A resounding message from both the millennial population and the business leaders surveyed was that the success of business should not be measured on profit alone and that the purpose of business cannot be defined in purely economic or financial terms. Profit as the sole measure of success is rejected by 92 percent of the millennials and 71 percent of business leaders."[189] The millennials and business leaders surveyed varied slightly on their perceptions of business purpose with over 50 percent of millennials citing innovation and societal development as primary, while business leader responses varied more widely to include profit and value. Connections between the groups can foster productive engagement. Thus, "[w]hile some of the differentiation may be accounted for by the relative idealism of youth and the relative experience and immediate pressures of leadership, the research does suggest that more clearly articulating and communicating the role business plays in pioneering innovation and driving societal development would enable today's business leaders to engage better with the central concerns of millennial talent."[190]

And while millennials may reflect more concentrated desires for social impact than more senior leaders, again we can think about fostering this intention, shared by most businesspeople, regardless of generational cohort, to expand the reach and impact of our organizations. The millennials can help us all actionalize these intentions. Harvard Business Review Press's *Passion & Purpose: Stories from the Best and Brightest Young Business Leaders* surveys 500 U.S. business school students whose discussions of motivation reflect the optimism and passion, sharing perspectives of MBAs who are entering business not only for financial gain, "but as a way to find meaningful work and make a positive difference in the world."[191] Reflecting on the aspirations of these young professionals can be inspirational for us all.

> The young do not know enough to be prudent and therefore they attempt the impossible—and achieve it, generation after generation. -Pearl S. Buck

Leveraging Purpose toward Organizational Effectiveness

Emerging professionals, their managers, and their organizations can engage in meaningful, fulfilling work. A key approach is leveraging employee strengths into organizational effectiveness. The *Giving Voice to Values* tenets of identifying and actualizing purpose, and translating values into effective decision making and action, can encourage us here. Aligning purpose, values, and leadership is not new; however, GVV contributes a practical approach that can be used by professionals at all levels. We thus know the *why* of values-based decision making at work, and GVV provides the *how*.

Giving Voice to Values explores those values that most people would agree have an ethical dimension to them—beyond qualities such as "innovation" and "creativity" or other important characteristics at work.[192] As discussed in Chapter 1, despite some differences, we can appeal to several characteristics as a helpful and manageable foundation. Sometimes called virtues, hypernorms, or core values, these characteristics include honesty, respect, responsibility, fairness, and compassion.[193] These widely held values provide guidance. Through intentional activities such as self-assessments, discussion of conflicts and exploration of relevant research and history, and other techniques, managers can consider values that they and others in their organization might share. Responses in research with 2,200 professionals across diverse industries asking what they desire in a workplace identified "strong values" as a key characteristic.[194] These findings reflect an expressed willingness to engage around values at work. Values discussions can thus provide a platform for professional development and employee impact.

Other studies also note this link between values identification and economic success. Thus, in contrast to most companies that begin determining strategy and direction by looking at markets and competition, "high-ambition" CEOs looked within the organization, and themselves, to determine "who" the company was to identify the most powerful intersection between their capabilities and purpose, and the passions of their people, with market opportunity.[195] This exploration reflects a clear alignment with notions of purpose. "These CEOs spent a great deal of time crystallizing their values and purpose and how strategy could be defined in a way that integrated strategy with values."[196] Success involves first "forging strategic identity"—another way to articulate purpose. Other findings related to characteristics of high-ambition leaders include the need for personal interaction with employees and transparent communication.[197] As we have acknowledged, millennials are primed to appreciate and respond to this approach.

> Engaging employees by defining purpose broadly and explicitly allows us to build and preserve our organizations. As the authors of *Conscious Capitalism: Liberating the Heroic Spirit of Business* remind us, "By embracing the idea that their primary, even sole purpose is to make money, businesses sacrifice the great power that comes from having a higher purpose. Worthy, transcendent goals elicit greater levels of creativity, collaboration, diligence, loyalty, and passion from all stakeholders."[198]

Another consideration is the value of work–life balance. Perhaps a helpful modification is to think of the issue as work–life *integration*.[199] Now before we run with arms flailing at the notion of even less time for personal considerations, perhaps we can again change the frame. If we consider the notion of integration—of our time, our values, our*selves*—this can open us to contributing to work in meaningful ways, to choosing and cultivating careers aligned with who we are and what we believe—in short, those characteristics expressly desired by millennials. This integration can be operationalized with alternative work schedules, child-care support, employee input into benefits and philanthropic activities, as just a few examples. This shift can be helpful for all professionals. Companies like Google and other "most valued" (and financially successful) firms offer some blueprints for these types of efforts. In big ways and small, we can think about better integrating our whole selves with what we do. That is the promise of GVV.

Articulating Purpose Within and Outside the Organization

Channeling employee desire for personal purpose into integration with professional and organizational values can be the province of a good manager, can lead to more engaged and productive employees, and can reduce the risk of ethical transgressions. Former Medtronic CEO and Harvard Business School thought leader Bill George uses the term "true north" to reflect this notion of an inner compass, or purpose at work, as a powerful tool. Self-reflection is a necessary first step—and when considering questions such as "What's the *purpose* of my leadership?" and "*Why* do I want to lead?" he notes that uncovering the answers may take decades. It is a work in progress, and one that requires self-assessment, a GVV pillar as a precursor to values-based decision making. Thus, "[l]eading is high stress work. There is no way to avoid the constant challenges of being responsible for people, organizations, outcomes, and uncertainties in the environment. Leaders who move up have greater freedom to control their destinies, but also experience increased pressure and seduction. Leaders can avoid these pitfalls by devoting themselves to personal development that cultivates their inner compass, or True North."[200]

This concept requires reframing leadership toward a model called servant leadership, requiring thought and introspection, and enables leaders to transition from seeking external satisfaction to internal satisfaction by making contributions—here we can recall our discussion of extrinsic versus intrinsic motivation. George goes on to note,

> The reality is that people cannot stay grounded by themselves. Leaders depend on people closest to them to stay centered. They should seek out people who influence them in profound ways and stay connected to them. Often their spouse or partner knows them best. They aren't impressed by titles, prestige, or wealth accumulation; instead, they worry that these outward symbols may be causing the loss of authenticity.

He also suggests a model similar to our peer- and leader mentoring discussed in Chapter 4, noting, "Spouses and partners can't carry this entire burden though. We need mentors to advise us when facing difficult decisions. Reliable mentors are entirely honest and straight with us, defining reality and developing action plans. In addition, intimate support groups, . . . with whom people can share their life experiences, hopes, fears, and challenges, are invaluable."[201]

These interactive, collaborative experiences, as we explored in Chapters 3 and 4, are critical for fostering organizational purpose. This reflection must be intentional, illustrating self-assessment and alignment, and the relationship between "knowing" and "doing." A McKinsey report on maximizing professional impact notes that "trying to change our behavior (what is seen and judged) will fail—the old, hard-wired patterns return when pressure mounts—unless we have first addressed internal patterns with conscious effort."[202] Creating time and place for peer-to-peer values conversations, scripting and practicing successful resolutions to ethical challenges, considering on the decisions of others, and other reflective practice allow leaders and their organizations to flourish.

Purpose as a focus can incorporate consideration of questions that can reinforce organizational goals. Such questions can include:

> What is a business's sense of purpose (shared identity and goals)? How and why did a particular business begin (imprinting effects of founding philosophies)? Who founded the enterprise and what did they want to achieve (entrepreneurial values, mission, and vision)? How does a sense of purpose relate to all the stakeholders in the organization and to the context in which it operates (stewardship and governance)? How does a business understand itself relative to society, and what is it doing to create a shared sense of purpose (institutional norms and logics)?[203]

Discussion of such issues with peers and colleagues can provide invaluable opportunities for growth and development. Companies that engage in this reflection and alignment with purpose are positioned to flourish.

Purpose at Work: Organizational Effectiveness

Other business stakeholders respond positively to this notion of corporate purpose. New research from the Aspen Institute reflects the perspective of investors, corporate leaders, and scholars on the purpose of the corporation, specifically those perspectives on the role of business in society. Respondents offered best practices and proposed solutions to combat short-term approaches to corporate accountability. Among those most frequently cited include altering incentive arrangements to align with longer-term goals; promoting the partnership between a clear and formal declaration of mission and a thorough alignment with that mission; fostering transparency by demanding better communication skills among corporate managers to counter the pernicious effects of short-term thinkers; creating better balance in the corporation's decision-making structure, particularly by expanding the influence of employees, whose well-being tends to be linked to long-term planning and success; demonstrating a greater commitment to attracting and training strong leaders; and increasing the visibility and exploiting the power of research that measures and evaluates corporate reputation.[204] Not surprisingly, these solutions align with the preferences and abilities of millennial talent. Companies can consider leveraging these skills toward goals that enhance the impact of the organization for all of its stakeholders.

How will this new paradigm emerge? Business schools are perfectly positioned to develop business leaders, investors, and other stakeholders who employ sound judgment, resist the allure of the short term, and help to realize the full potential of the corporation. In this post-Enron, almost-post-financial crisis era, we must consider a fuller understanding of long-term value creation. As noted in a report from the Aspen Institute Business & Society Program, "While financial surplus is certainly one vital sign of corporate health, it offers little insight into the ability of a corporation to create financial and other forms of value in the future."[205] Companies face changes in market forces, public sentiment, consumer and labor pressure, and legislative approaches that attempt to align corporate capacities with the long-term health of society.[206]

Thus, "[the questions that arise from this new paradigm for business] call for new, broader thinking about corporate purpose, how we define and measure risk and value creation in business, how we measure the performance of corporate leaders, how we distribute the rewards for increased corporate productivity, and how we improve accountability, incentives, and regulation." The report notes the role of business education in equiping emerging leaders. "In exploring questions of corporate purpose more deeply in their research and the classroom, business faculty can shape MBAs into leaders able to more fully realize the vast potential of the corporation, both for their own success and for the long-term health of society."[207] The notion of applied knowledge is again key—business schools can "put more emphasis on doing rather than telling, giving students experience [through internships or other experiential learning], working in situations that force them to examine their ethics and act on them."[208]

I am fortunate to witness these approaches in actions at my university. Student interest and participation in social entrepreneurship programs, including courses, internships, and the launch of new ventures, is exploding. Students are hungry for opportunities to utilize their business skills toward social impact. We see young entrepreneurs starting new ventures in developing countries in need of clean, sustainable water sources, repurposing shipping materials into safe and affordable housing, and myriad other applications. Students work in collaboration with entrepreneurs in their own communities around the world to scale up and enhance economic vitality and services. Their enthusiasm is inspiring and contagious. Emerging professionals are jumping in feet first to create shared value.

The concept of shared value, first introduced by Porter and Kramer, focuses on the connections between economic and societal progress, and provides a lens for the modern corporation to view decisions and opportunities. These opportunities need not be direct community impact programs, though the evidence that such efforts pay dividends is great. Ethical practices can take many forms, and identifying these opportunities can be enhanced through engagement with young professionals. The resulting innovations and growth will benefit both companies and society. Through practices that enhance the competitiveness of a company while simultaneously advancing the economic and social conditions in the communities in which it operates, both the company and society can prosper:

Not all profit is equal—an idea that has been lost in the narrow, short-term focus of financial markets and in much management thinking. Profits involving a social purpose represent a higher form of capitalism—one that will enable society to advance more rapidly while allowing companies to grow even more. The result is a positive cycle of company and community prosperity, which leads to profits that endure.[209]

Companies can identify, with strategic thinking, and with the perspective of young talent for whom creating social value is likely front of mind, those opportunities to create shared value that make sense in their industry. Shared value opportunities are closely related to a company's industry and business; in that space, companies can benefit financially and sustain commitments over time, and bring the most resources to bear with scale and market presence equipping them to meaningfully impact a societal problem.[210] Porter and Kramer (2011) offer additional suggestions and tips for strategic integration of this approach that are well worth exploring.

These opportunities for impact can come from even our youngest stakeholders. The *Wall Street Journal* recently profiled an effort by Royal DSM in North America to engage employees around social impact using an unexpected driver—the annual, and ubiquitous, "take our daughters and sons to work day." A group of young people, children of employees, developed persuasive presentations to share with executives on social causes the company could impact. Featuring such topics as providing solar cooking stoves to schools in sub-Saharan Africa to allow more girls to attend, to focusing on food shortages in other parts of the developing world, the young people present compelling information around corporate engagement. Aside from being wowed by the technical acumen reflected in the presentations, which included embedded video, music tracks, and live chats with experts in remote locations, employees were motivated to implement projects and develop an ongoing collaboration with the group. The collaboration involves other engagement, including seeking other feedback from the group—the executives, for example, have asked what the young people think of their parents' work schedule. "Their responses helped prompt DSM to implement flexible summer hours and remote working. The youngsters' multimedia skills are also in demand. . . . [with] some senior administrative assistants [approaching] the group after its PowerPoint presentation, trying to garner tips for when their bosses might ask them to match the kids' jazzy presentation skills." One executive noted, "I wanted to hire some of them on the spot"".[211]

Here we can consider another suggestion posited by one of our emerging professionals:

[Companies could] institute new team-building days and activities built around increasing company and community sustainability. Having days where employees can get out of the office and engage in team building exercises can do wonders for both internal cohesiveness and productivity. In addition, the fact that employees are being given a chance to impact some issue that they may care deeply about will help raise their opinions of the organization they work for and improve morale. These events would be company-wide and would be set up by a new team established for this specific purpose. All employees are encouraged to submit ideas for team-building days (MM student).

Finally, to again take our cues from best practices in academic learning, we can consider tips for enhancing learning outcomes in a variety of contexts. The best college professors frame academic learning around the "big questions"—what are the questions we are trying to answer? What is the goal of what we are doing?—rather than rote understanding of concepts and skills.[212] Millennials are primed for this interest in aligning purpose with their work. I have never seen my own students more engaged than when we are working in the field, applying business skills to addressing social concerns. For example, our undergraduate seniors advise youth entrepreneurs as they design business plans, develop accounting, volunteer and donor management programs for staff of an advocacy center, and assist with job preparation programs at a center for women in need. I have never seen them more passionate than when they are engaged in discussions on their desire to bring their gifts, talents, and curious minds to work. This enthusiasm and desire for purpose can be cultivated and channeled. Managers can incorporate explicit discussion of organizational mission, and personal and professional purpose, to maximize outcomes for all stakeholders.

Chapter 5: Action Items

Purpose at work, explicitly and broadly defined, can be a powerful galvanizing issue for employees—millennials and management alike. Here are several strategies millennials and their managers might consider to embrace purpose toward organizational effectiveness.

(1) Acknowledge that the nature of work is changing to reflect non-routine, innovative, and dynamic tasks—*the "carrot and stick" of extrinsic motivation no longer suffices for effective engagement of our employees.* Motivation must incorporate notions of purpose to maximize contributions and effectiveness.

(2) *Managers do well to acknowledge the expressed desires of millennial talent to connect their work with meaning.* This does not mean they cannot or will not do repetitious or taxing work—but rather that connections with the "big picture" of mission and goals, and engagement around the work at hand, are key.

(3) *Recognize that explicit considerations of meaning and purpose can benefit the leaders themselves, and employees at all levels of the organization.* Creating space for articulating purpose and values at work can be the province of effective managers who acknowledge the connections between meaning and professional success.

(4) *Consider notions of shared value and broad conceptions of wealth creation.* Creating viable businesses, reflecting sustainable, ethical success, can involve young talent driving connections with opportunities for impact and engagement, with triple-bottom-line benefits for the organization.

CHAPTER 6

The Millennials Speak

All photographs used with permission, Copyright © 2014
by Della Dewald

All photographs used with permission, Copyright © 2014
by Della Dewald

All photographs used with permission,
Copyright © 2014 by Della Dewald

Emerging research on the perspectives of young talent and on managing millennials, along with highlights from our own conversations with these up-and-coming businesspeople, can help guide our efforts to maximize impact toward ethical, effective organizations. We interviewed a group of 22 senior business students and surveyed 138 more business sophomores, juniors and seniors at a top U.S. business school to learn from their perceptions and aspirations. My hope is that these findings, along with results from other research exploring the perspectives of emerging and new business professionals, can assist managers in building connections with this young talent.

In addition, we can consider some specific suggestions of effective approaches to managing millennials for ethical leadership from a representative group of these young people themselves. Their perspectives have been integrated throughout our exploration. Thus, 75 students in my course called *Managing and Millennials* were asked to design fictional management programs for engaging millennial and multigenerational talent as a culminating assignment in a course dedicated to these topics. Students were asked to consider their own preferences for workplace solutions, based on their values and desired activities at work, and to include reference to researched best practices in millennial management. Their suggestions are illuminating and reflect many of the approaches we have explored in this book. Highlights are included throughout the book as suggestions companies may wish to consider. We will start by acknowledging the context in which generational differences are often framed. We will review some of these issues and then turn to millennial perspectives, in their own words.

Contextual Issues for Millennials in Business

For just one timely example, "job-hopping" or lack of loyalty is a charge often levied at millennial talent, but a close look at the statistics may uncover that economic instability accounts for much of the reported high numbers of positions of young professionals. These young people are also entering the workforce with unprecedented student debt—a weight that clearly impacts job choice. Researchers found that younger millennials, those who witnessed the recession of the 2000s, express increasing concern for others and less interest in material goods, reversing a trend that had held for nearly four decades. "This data reflects a broader pattern. Between 1976 and 2010, high school seniors expressed more concern for others during times of economic hardship, and less concern for others during times of economic prosperity. During times of hardship, young people more frequently look outward to others and the world at large."[213] The author goes on to note that, of course, we are dealing with challenging economic times, but that perhaps this contributes to a specific benefit: "Millennials have been forced to reconsider what a successful life constitutes. By focusing on making a positive difference in the lives of others, rather than on more materialistic markers of success, they are setting themselves up for the meaningful life they yearn to have."[214]

The economic conditions may in fact enable millennials to be more selective in their career choices—because so many are un- and underemployed, and living at home with parents, the stigma of these conditions seems to be lessened. Millennials may benefit from their parents' willingness to provide financial support much longer than in previous generations, and thus have the flexibility to pursue work that they find meaningful. If they do not perceive that their need for connection and purpose is met at a specific company, they will seek it elsewhere.

Another contextual factor the millennials face is the myriad and often contradictory messages from the academic, professional, and peer communities that inundate them in this age of information. They desire impact and meaning, and in this era there are many different paths toward these goals. They are simultaneously told that they are narcissistic, then faulted for trying to forge their identities in ways that resonate with meaning and values as they have been encouraged to do since they were quite young.

In addition, companies would do well to recognize a variety of perspectives are being shared with young talent, and that these networked young people are deluged with these messages from many corners. We have already acknowledged some of the dynamics of their formative years. We can also consider, for example, the advice they are getting from some successful young professionals, who offer career development guidance that is absolutely counter to the messages older workers may have received early in their job-seeking days. For instance, one young entrepreneur notes, in a LinkedIn post "recommended" by over 1,000 readers within one day of the post going online:

> Going to work at a start-up or growth company in your 20s will put you on the fast-lane learning curve. It will be the best investment you can make because *you'll find yourself*. The folks who have come into [this author's startup] in their 20s unclear about their passions, often emerge knowing who they are—becoming business development people or founders or product managers or people managers. They *find their calling fast* because the pace of the business requires it. You might be concerned about what happens if your start-up fails. Relax. You (probably) don't have kids at home. You can always move into your friend's crappy one bedroom apartment for a couple of months. And I promise you this—the most employable person in the tech industry is the highly motivated 25 year old (ideally with technical skills). So even if that start-up doesn't work out, don't worry—*you'll have plenty of other opportunities and a clear sense of yourself* (emphasis mine).[215]

This post reflects a sentiment we are increasingly hearing—finding a calling is a priority in a way that finding a "job" just is not. As one author notes, "today's elite graduates . . . no longer look to Wall Street as the be-all, end-all of a gainful and challenging first career. Instead, many have turned to the allure of Silicon Valley—and who can blame them? The promise of the tech world, in a nutshell, is that working slightly better hours in jeans and a T-shirt, with snacks and a football table at the ready, will be more fun and every bit as lucrative as banking."[216]

What Do Millennials Want at Work—and Are We Meeting the Challenge?

What do these young professionals really hope to offer, and receive at work? As we have acknowledged, interaction and input are key, and research suggests that both are under-acknowledged in many companies. For example, despite the expressed nature of millennials to prefer clear and consistent communication about expectations for performance, many managers fail to set expectations, performance indicators, and criteria for promotions, and conduct regular and substantive performance reviews—a recent study found that one in five managers do not provide annual reviews.[217] When managers do not invest in young talent and help them uncover their path, they look elsewhere (which costs firms an average of $24,000 per employee).[218]

Talent managers also note that the traditional approach to career maturation and promotion has been accelerated. Thus, some experts suggest fast-tracking successful performers as a necessary step for today's companies:

> If you take the long view, it makes sense to prepare your best, young professionals now for the big promotional step that their predecessors typically had to wait 10, 15 years or longer to expect. They're already so 'up to speed' on so many essential, differentiating aspects of the competitive marketplace that they add value now that renders the typical career maturing process obsolete.[219]

Failure to acknowledge this dynamic can be detrimental: "You want to keep them. And to keep them often means promoting them at a more accelerated rate than you might have normally."[220]

Yet, of course, this does not mean these young upstarts are without need for development, and, encouragingly, indications are that they recognize that they need this extra support in critical areas. A 2014 study of over 400 millennial managers, their managers, peer managers, team members, and HR and business leaders found that all groups agree that millennials need extra support in several areas: establishing respect and credibility that will enable them to lead older team members, building fundamental skills that are conventionally learned through natural progression of long careers, understanding effective and efficient work, and doing all of these things "while acknowledging hierarchy, bureaucracy, and status quo, and allow[ing] for the necessary patience and time for projects and ideas to mature and gain coalition among a variety of constituents necessary to ensure the success that everyone desires."[221] This finding also echoes our earlier consideration of engaged and connected cultures resonating with ethical and sustainable success.

The research team in the 2014 study developed specific suggestions to support senior executives in developing millennial leaders, including raising the millennials' visibility internally with specific communication and development initiatives to ensure their acceptance by the entire organization, and leveraging their eagerness to learn from real-time, "on the go" coaching spurts: "The time it takes to walk down the hallway with your millennials could be just enough time to offer praise for a job well done, a quick tip, action step, or insight that will help them improve their performance the next time."[222]

These researchers also reinforce several of the tips we have explored, such as explicitly bridging the generation "gap" by explicitly acknowledging the challenges to intergenerational work and focusing on finding common ground, by encouraging innovative thinking, including allowing new ideas to be presented and to working alongside millennials to help bring ideas into solid business implementation, and by revisiting expectations about how and when work best gets done. To this last point, research suggests that 69 percent of millennials believe that regular office attendance is unnecessary, "And they may actually be right. Take a fresh look at how your work gets done, and whether being present in one's permanently assigned cubicle really is essential to productivity and effectiveness. You may return to the conclusion that a conventional 9-to-5 schedule works best for your company. But a fresh study of scheduling assumptions will help you articulate your reasoning when your millennials ask you why—and they will."[223] These are all steps toward more engaged, collaborative workplaces—those in which millennials can flourish, and in which connected, ethical cultures will thrive.

The 2014 team ends the report with a reminder that the training and development of millennial talent is a collaborative effort on the part of young people and their managers:

All indications point to the principle that companies that want to stay fast and nimble in their marketplace must be willing to fast-track their young high-performers into essential leadership roles. This is good strategy. Just never lose sight of the fact that they will need that extra support as they help your company race to the top.[224]

This emphasis on coaching and collaborative learning helps cultivate this talent in positive ways, toward effective, ethical business.

Finally, as the millennials with whom we spoke were quick to point out, exploring context includes acknowledging why millennial characteristics emerged as they have. Thus, who raised these young people? What were the visions and goals of their parents for their children? (Or, as one of our respondents noted, only half-kidding: "Who created these monsters?") We suspect that these goals for our young people include meaning, contentedness, satisfaction, connection, and feelings of contribution—all admirable goals. Let us not lament them in their conviction that success and happiness are not mutually exclusive.

Values at Work: Critical to Millennial Engagement

Research indicates the following among the top five characteristics millennials want in a boss: Help with navigating their career paths, straight feedback, mentoring and coaching, and formal professional development (supervisor comfort with flexible schedules rounds out the list).[225] When asked what they want from their companies, they indicated a preference for an organization that will develop employees' skills and one with "strong values" among their top responses. The *Giving Voice to Values* (GVV) approach directs these inclinations into effective skill development, because of course these inclinations must be channeled realistically and toward shared goals. This practical consideration is important, as at this point some of us may be reflecting a response echoed here: "'Oh, they want total fulfillment?' managers maybe thinking. 'Is *that* all?'" This, however, can be framed as a strength:

> Yes, Millennials have high expectations of their employers—but they also set high standards for themselves. They've been working on their résumés practically since they were toddlers, because there are so many of them and so few (relatively speaking) spots at top schools and top companies. They're used to overachieving academically and to making strong personal commitments to

community service. *Keep them engaged, and they will be happy to overachieve for you.*[226] (emphasis mine)

Again here we can consider the critical role of business education in the formation of these young leaders, and the need for ongoing attention to these issues in the workplace. Leveraging their inclinations toward creating social and environmental value through business can allow emerging leaders to help shape our businesses toward triple-bottom-line success. This approach resonates with millennials and their role in organizations. This realization echoes effective business education, specifically, education that prompts discernment of values and their role in the professions. Sims and Felton (2006) reflect the importance of this integration of learning and living:

> The learning process has two core goals. One is to learn the content of a particular subject matter like business ethics. The other is to learn one's own strengths and weaknesses as a learner. When the process works well, students finish their ethics learning experience with not only new intellectual insights but also new understandings of their own learning style.

An approach incorporating self-awareness and alignment is a core GVV tenant, recognizing that self-assessment is a precursor to values alignment in professional decision making. These scholars go on to note,

> It has been our experience that this understanding of learning strengths and weaknesses helps in the application of what has been learned to real-world situations and provides a framework for continued learning. In this instance, learning is no longer a special activity reserved for the classroom; it becomes an integral and explicit part of the work world business students will encounter upon graduation.[227]

Managers can reinforce this notion of the workplace as a space for growth and development.

In one major national study, 65 percent of graduating students indicate their belief that they will make a positive social or environmental

Table 6.1 Most important values in planning future employment

(Please rank the following from most important to you (1) to least important (9) regarding importance as you plan future employment in the business realm. (n = 138))

Answer options	Rating average
The type of work I do matches my interests and skills	3.11
Family/work balance and flexible schedule	3.88
Opportunities for advancement	3.99
High salary and good benefits	4.02
The company has a high standard of ethics	5.23
The company is located near where I want to live	5.49
Opportunities for training and development	5.64
The product or service the company produces is important to me	5.95
The company has high standards of environmental responsibility	7.7

impact through their work, and 58 percent indicate, with all else equal, they would take a 15 percent pay cut to work for an organization with values that align with their own.[228] This aligns with our student survey of a subset of these young graduates, where the majority of students reflected the sentiment of this young woman: *"I want to be happy doing whatever I enjoy. If my job is high-paying, yet I am miserable every day at work, I will find something that better suits my interests."* We saw that these perspectives reflected consistently.

These responses resonate with other research on millennial professionals, with interest alignment, flexibility, and opportunities for advancement as top desires. An interesting and telling note merits attention here as well. In the space provided for additional comments regarding this survey question, many students noted their concern that these items are listed as mutually exclusive, which is misleading; rather, most of these values are quite important to them. This discomfort with a "forced ranking" may be indicative of a desire to "have it all" and reflect the desire to achieve personal and professional fulfillment without sacrifice or compromise. Future research could explore how these responses might change over the course of one's career.

My own students talk about these issues in class, and in our one-on-one discussions—often! They are excited, nervous, optimistic, and anxious—and ultimately, very hopeful—as they embark on their careers. They want to make their mark, to be happy, and to create positive impact—and most of them clearly recognize, and have already begun signaling, that hard work is required for all of the above. I am optimistic about the future of our businesses whenever I speak with my business students.

We can then acknowledge another aspect of desired work characteristics. Much discussion of millennials focuses on their motivations—why they do what they do. Research in motivation at work reminds us that most everyone in our organizations responds well to the dynamics of motivation explicitly preferred by millennial talent. Thus, recognizing and operationalizing intrinsic motivation, related to "autonomy (the desire to direct our own lives), mastery (the urge to make progress and get better at something that matters), and purpose (the yearning to do what we do in the service of something larger than ourselves)"[229], is critical for high-performing organizations. Not surprisingly, these are also considerations required for effective, ethical decision making.

As one young professional notes in an article called "Message From a Millennial," millennials can be part of a paradigm change at work that will benefit our organizations at every level:

We've spent so much time sitting in classrooms and reading textbooks learning about revolutions—people sticking up for their rights as workers and as human beings demanding better treatment and a better environment. So why would we just grin and bear the conditions we've been given? There is always room for improvement. After all, your generation and the generations before you taught us that. We want to continue to stand up for our rights, this time for work-life balance and for increasing the love we have for what we do.[230]

Millennial Ownership of Impact and Image

Millennials, of course, are not exempt from responsibility in this new paradigm. Rather, young professionals must manage their professional presence deliberately and consistently. An expert on young professionals at work offers advice to "have a plan, measure yourself, and communicate often,"[231] noting that these business fundamentals have not changed with the tide of millennials rising. Specifically, technology can certainly be used to increase flexibility and productivity, but face time still matters—supplementing e-mail responsiveness with face-to-face interactions in person or via video is a great way to stay front of mind. In addition, measuring success can be a challenge in today's environment outside of sales and other budget-related metrics, so young talent should consider creating detailed plans and reporting on progress—measuring activities and also measuring results. This reporting aligns well with millennials' achievement orientation and penchant for measuring and tracking results (for evidence, just consider the success of lifestyle tracking, fitness tracking, friendship tracking, and other metrics inherent to millennials' technologically enhanced lives). Millennials can translate use of these these metrics to professional impact. Cates (2014) notes, "Don't give anyone room to question your dedication to your work."[232]

Much is made in many business schools about "personal brands"—a business-speak translation of the idea of personal and professional distinction and purpose. Explicitly considering one's "mission statement" extends the natural progression of motivated young professionals who project their images online through tools like LinkedIn (which reports nearly 260 million users worldwide, and is the 12th most visited web site in the world). We include the "Personal and Professional Profile" (Appendix B) as a tool that can help guide this self-assessment.

Finally, we should again acknowledge that the influence of values and purpose as drivers are part and parcel for millennials; the manner in which these are expressed merits consideration. We see this dynamic reflected in the ways they engage with their work and with social issues they believe in, and in how they communicate with others. For example, a study of over 16,000 millennials regarding their connections with social causes found that "these young do-gooders are quickly influencing how [social service] organizations communicate to all audiences. Marketing and messaging will lend itself more to the millennial style of communication, with an emphasis on authentic stories and visual presentations that are concise, mobile-friendly, and delivered online via social media platforms."[233] Over the four years of this particular study, millennials only increased their attraction to using imagery and video for learning about social causes, and their preference for using mobile technology for information and communication. They are also invaluable in spreading the word about a cause or issue—this unofficial marketing role contributes to grassroots and other movements—a change from previous generations. The connections also seem to be with causes and relationships, and not with the helping organizations themselves, a dynamic we see in the corporate arena as well. As with other areas of involvement, immediacy reigns—millennials are hungry for "vicariously experienc[ing] social needs and see[ing] how their small action can help alleviate a need in that moment."[234] Companies may wish to consider how to translate these proclivities and skills toward organizational goals, such as communicating values, engendering support for core initiatives, and other strategic processes.

Millennial Voice

These considerations can return us to specific consideration of fostering ethical impact. As discussed in previous chapters, positively affecting our organizations by effectively voicing values requires first acknowledging that there are many different ways to "speak." As noted in Chapter 3, a significant issue in intergenerational collaboration is the method by which we express ourselves, not necessarily the content of the message. This dynamic includes communication of values at work. Our values can be expressed in numerous ways; some may work better than others in particular contexts. Each of us may be more comfortable with, skilled at, or likely to use one approach over another; thus, in the context of values challenges, our ability to see a way to use that particular approach can be a critical determining factor as to *whether* we speak. Some organizational contexts, conditions, and types of leaders will have a significant impact on our own and others' likelihood of voicing values. Millennials and their managers can undertake activities to make it more likely that we will express our values and that we will do so effectively—specifically, practice and coaching.[235] This can be the province of effective personal and organizational professional development.

GVV provides exploration of key techniques to assist millennials and their managers in developing their capacities around ethical decision making, enhancing this voice and making it more likely we will act in accordance with our personal and organizational values. Business professionals can incorporate explicit discussion of these dynamics, in collaboration with peers and colleagues. Incorporating such discussions, case studies, and other exercises into workshops and trainings normalizes ethical concerns at work, and allows for employees to explore corporate and personal values made real. This interaction around values, engaging and action-oriented, is a great fit with millennial inclinations.

Thus, a critical area of attention in these values considerations concerns recognizing familiar categories of argument or reasons for the defense of ethically questionable behavior. In addition, there are useful questions, persuasive arguments, and ways of framing information that can help us respond effectively to these common arguments; in our consideration of cultivating millennial voice, it is helpful to explore them.

First, and importantly, the very act of "naming" an argument in favor of ethically questionable behavior, perhaps in the context of discussing cases based on previous personal or organizational experience, can acknowledge that such a tactic can reduce its power—we have made it discussable and subject to equal, or hopefully stronger, counter-arguments. *Choice,* whether or not to act, becomes possible—the fundamental tenet of the GVV approach.[236] Cultivating this awareness is useful for personal development and for professional capacity building. It also fosters self-efficacy, a millennial goal for their professional life.

These common categorizations or patterns of ethical dilemmas are outlined in more detail in Chapter 7 and in the GVV curriculum; we consider highlights here as useful discussion topics, or reflection opportunities, at work. Thus, common patterns often used to frame ethical dilemmas include "truth versus loyalty, individual versus community, short-term versus long-term, and justice versus mercy"[237]. These "false dichotomies" often offered to us are misrepresentations and are frequently employed as a form of rationalization for unethical decision making. Sometimes values conflicts only appear to be such "right versus right" dilemmas due to the way they are framed, ignoring the "wrong" that may be there.

As an example of a "false dichotomy," we can consider this example. A colleague may appeal to personal loyalty in order to persuade us to go along with an unethical reporting tactic—do not let "the team" down—presenting his appeal as a dilemma of "truth" (honest reporting) versus "loyalty" (prioritizing the material welfare of the team). With preparation, we can see this as the rationalization that it is, and begin to formulate a response. We can consider what is truly loyal—which is likely that decision that acknowledges the long-term integrity of the group. One needs to only revisit the Enron debacle to witness the destruction a misguided appeal to loyalty can engender. Sims and Brinkmann (2003) note,

> Enron's culture [was] a good example of groupthink . . . where individuals feel extreme pressure not to express any real strong arguments against any coworkers' actions. Although very individualistic, the culture at Enron was at the same conformist. . . . Employees were loyal in an ambiguous sense of the term, i.e. they wanted to be seen as part of the start team and to partake in the benefits that that honor entailed. . . . Loyalty required . . . [that employees] 'keep drinking the Enron water.'[238]

A similar dynamic characterized the inexcusable cover-up of unacceptable behavior in the Penn State child abuse scandal: "Loyalty that hides problematic conduct is a false loyalty, for it elevates reputation over reality, and esteems image over character. Though we may believe we are acting to protect the institution, in reality we do the institution and individuals far greater damage—even if the deceit is never discovered."[239] Familiarizing ourselves with these common categories of values conflicts allows us to clearly consider whether the nature and spirit of the values at issue—loyalty, truth, mercy, justice, and so on—are truly relevant, and ascribed appropriately, to the given dilemma.[240]

Additionally, we often encounter categories of argument or rationalization for unethical behaviors; with exploration, we can become more adept at responding to them effectively. Managers can broach these topics generally, through cases and perhaps using lived experiences, to vividly engage employees around discussion of taking action in accordance with our values. For example, we could discuss the common appeal to "expected practice" ("*everyone is doing it*"), recognizing that this is often an exaggeration—if the practice were truly accepted, why are there rules, laws, or policies against it?[241] Discussing these and other frequent categories of rationalization, and specific strategies to confront them, can be used to develop our "muscle" for responding to ethical challenges. When considered in the context of professional development, they can be powerful discussion prompts for millennials and their managers—and for all members of connected workplaces. Thus, we consider categories of argument and rationalization, along with categories of values dilemmas, to help us recognize them, understand the ways of thinking that produce them, and to be practiced in responding to them.[242] Doing this together, with our millennials and our colleagues, can be powerful prompts for acknowledging voice and positive impact at work.

Chapter 6: Action Items

Research on the perspectives of young talent and on managing millennials, along with exploring their goals and concerns in their own words, can inform our efforts to maximize impact toward successful, ethical businesses. Examining these perspectives can assist managers in connecting with and developing these young professionals. Below are several considerations that may be helpful.

(1) *Managers can acknowledge that millennials are facing myriad, and often conflicting, messages about the role of work in their lives, are seeking employment in a new and challenging context, and grew up with expectations and experiences that shape who they are.* Coming-of-age amidst financial and political uncertainty, facing unprecedented debt and national recession, and raised by parents who have spent more time with them than any generation before, millennials value engaged workplaces that foster feelings of involvement and allow for meaningful impact. The workplace can be a critical space for impact and connections, and investments in true connection can pay dividends in commitment and productivity.

(2) *Millennials recognize the need for and respond to training and development, perhaps more so than previous generations.* They are hungry for professional development they feel is relevant and meaningful; opportunities for this growth should be framed in a way to recognize impact and significance. Managers can leverage this willingness to grow and flourish, engaging young talent around development of ethical, effective organizations by active coaching and by incorporating notions of purpose and impact.

(3) *Millennials display strong levels of interest in creating social and environmental value through business; managers can leverage these inclinations toward triple-bottom-line success.* Young talent is poised to contribute to organizations that will thrive in this era of resounding calls for prosocial corporate impact. Engaging millennials in meaningful contribution toward organizational strategies and goals can

help us build companies willing and able to meet the challenges and opportunities of our globalized, connected world.

(4) *Millennials have new responsibilities in this new paradigm of connection and access; young professionals must manage their professional presence deliberately and consistently.* Managers would do well to acknowledge these dynamics explicitly with young employees, and discuss how they contribute to professional success.

(5) *Managers can leverage available tools to assist in developing the capacities of employees around ethical decision making.* Business professionals can incorporate explicit discussion of dynamics that make it more likely employees will act in accordance with personal and organizational values, and can engage in these explorations in collaboration with peers and colleagues. Discussions, case studies, and other exercises can be incorporated into workshops and trainings to normalize ethical concerns at work, and allow for employees to explore corporate and personal values made real. This engaging and action-oriented interaction around values is a great fit with millennial inclinations.

CHAPTER 7

Corporate Best Practices

All photographs used with permission,
Copyright © 2014 by Della Dewald

Chapter 7 presents an overview of considerations for organizations interested in strengthening productive, ethical cultures through engagement
with millennial talent. As noted, the specific strategies and approaches of
organizational leadership have tremendous influence over the outcomes
and impact of young talent in our businesses. I hope that the strategies
provided throughout this book will be helpful in formulating and supporting your own innovative initiatives. We conclude our exploration of
managing millennials with this chapter, highlighting specific corporate
examples for illustration and inspiration. We will start by examining

research highlights that provide useful insights, and then look to several corporate approaches that illustrate effective strategies.

Thus, should corporations adapt to meet the needs of the millennial generation? Of course, to some extent, all successful organizations incorporate some level of accommodation and development to meet contextual factors such as market demand and changes in the talent pipeline. Importantly, the task of effectively managing millennials toward personal and organizational flourishing must involve both these young professionals and those who lead them working together. Some scholars have criticized the "coddling" of millennials' "special needs" that some organizations adopt to attract and retain young talent. These scholars suggest focusing on competency development rather than other approaches (no jacuzzis in the break room here).

For example, a competency-focused approach may include mechanisms such as gainsharing, a pay-for-performance model that incorporates the notion of "common fate" in which rewards are associated with achievement of organizational goals, to maximize millennial impact.[243] These models can be quite effective in certain contexts and do much to create shared accountability and reward. However, like most financial performance-driven compensation systems, they require careful management to avoid lapses into ethically questionable means to achieve organizational (and personal) ends. These authors make an important point. "Coddling" is certainly not effective for either the young professional or their company. Yet strategies in addition to the "carrot" of financial incentives can be even more effective and feasible for managers and other leaders.

Thoughtful incorporation of practices designed to maximize ethical and organizational impact of all employees is required. We can start by considering techniques that leverage the strengths of these young professionals, in the context of multigenerational work cultures, toward more successful, ethical organizations for all. A new business paradigm can emerge from exploring the gifts and challenges of this generation, the ways that they reflect the opportunities in today's business environment, and how companies can prosper.

Thus, "employee-friendly" policies need not be synonymous with management headaches, increased costs, and coddling of millennial workers. Company-wide policies that are motivated by the expressed desires of the millennial generation can benefit the organization as a whole. With explicit and careful attention, managers can design and implement programs and policies tailored to the unique needs of their organizations, and that reflect the types of approaches utilized by successful organizations in every context and industry. Thus, programs can have broad appeal, such as parental leave, child care, and wellness, stress reduction, and other employee assistance programs; others may target a select group of the workplace with approaches such as adoption assistance, domestic partner benefits, leave and job shares, and exit and re-entry opportunities, while some approaches, such as flextime, may be possible in larger organizations, but less desirable or impossible those that are smaller: "Managers can fashion options designed around employee preferences that can bring positive payoff in terms of worker productivity, morale, retention, and job commitment. Failing to give attention to these matters can have reverse effects."[244]

In many cases, we have work to do in illustrating that positive attention to these challenges results in a significant return on investment (financial and otherwise) at work. One respondent in our survey of corporate managers reflected a level of frustration shared by several others:

"The problem is that companies are bending over backward to accommodate [millennials]. There have been additional offerings of reduced work schedules and flowery communications to "entice" Gen Y. Companies are wasting financial resources when the message should be 'Gen Y, work hard like your grandparents and you will earn your success.'"

This frustration, likely rooted in personal experience, reflects a perception that young talent must acknowledge. Students in our study reflected this awareness and acknowledge it as a challenge to overcome. Several indicated feeling that they were fighting negative perceptions from day one in internship and work experiences, with one student commenting (to nods of agreement around the room filled with young people):

"Before [my supervisor] even met me he just thought 'here's this young know-it-all'. . . . You come in automatically as a 'millennial' with this stamp on your head and [others believe] 'you didn't earn what you have' . . . or that you're trying to be a know-it-all with all the answers. . . . So much of my work was trying to get that stamp off my forehead. . . . People have this preconceived notion of you just because you're young."

When asked how he dealt with these perceptions, he noted,

"You just let your actions take over—they speak louder than words . . . If you're working hard and performing well, well then they'll just say, 'Okay, he can run with the old bucks.' . . . [Millennials] just have to really try to work and be hyper aware and show [older colleagues] that [their perceptions] are not the case."

Many students in our study reacted strongly to perceived stereotyping of their generation, and blame social media in part for this negative attention. One student noted,

"There are definitely millennials who have those characteristics [of narcissism and laziness]. . . . The ability of our generation to take advantage of social media means that the people who otherwise would not have a platform to showcase their laziness, selfishness or narcissism suddenly have a way to reach a lot of people. I think that if other generations had the same platforms then they would have had the same results."

Here again is an opportunity for managers and employees to acknowledge these dynamics within our organizations, and engage in explicit conversation about them. This chapter provides some suggestions.

To signal and reinforce our optimism toward millennials at work, we also asked these young people to describe their perceptions of the strengths of millennial talent. We were pleased to see these results align nicely with employer perceptions of these strengths—both groups identified technological fluency, comfort with diversity, values orientations, flexibility, willingness to adapt to changes, and enthusiasm as among their strengths. Inserting these topics into discussion among employees and with management can help change the frame from laments to fostering positive contribution.

Setting the Stage for Effective, Ethical Cultures

An additional note on best practices is key. As we have acknowledged throughout this volume, effective leadership in today's business requires considering the intersection between effective and ethical cultures. Because of the alignment with this generation's capacities and inclinations, and the global, sustainable nature of business, it is perhaps not surprising that the best practices for engaging millennials at work align well with strategies for success in fostering ethical, successful organizations that can flourish in the modern environment.

Eisner (2012) offers recommended general best practices to frame an approach to effectively managing millennials, which include several features, some specific to fostering ethical cultures, including flattening the organization, leading by example and transparency, mentoring and coaching, operationalizing work–life balance, acknowledging and celebrating, and facilitating making a difference.[245]

We have explored these general guidelines in previous chapters; in addition, we can examine specific opportunities for fostering ethical, effective companies. A recent report from Deloitte suggests specific steps for organizations to move from "good enough" to "great" ethics and compliance programs—a progression that is necessary in this era of increased risks due to social media, mobile technologies, and big data, and that has been demanded by U.S. Federal Sentencing Guidelines and other regulatory efforts, and even more significantly, by key stakeholders in business. Enhanced transparency means that these programs are accessible to employees, consumers, investors, and society at large, and the organizations that will be most successful are those that pursue ethics strategies with several key characteristics[246]:

- careful attention to tone at the top;
- a corporate culture that reflects compliance and integrity;
- risk assessments that account for changing landscapes and allow for focused attention;
- testing and monitoring to help ensure that the control environment is effective;
- a skilled and supported chief ethics and compliance officer.

Denis Collins (2009) offers clear and actionable resources for companies interested in implementing best practices in ethics management, including risk management and performance quality benchmarking tools, and specific tips for reinforcing ethical behavior.[247] Starting by rating your business against best practices in ethical leadership can provide a specific agenda for enhancing performance across the organization. These best practices align well with millennial characteristics, skills, and expressed desires for work environments. Tips include *ethics screens during hiring,* explicit *attention to ethics and values in orientation,* annual *ethics and diversity training* in the spirit of continuous improvement, establishment of *an ethical reporting system, reinforcement of ethics through work goals and performance appraisals* that reward ethical behaviors and punish those that are unethical, fostering a sense of organizational ownership through *team-based participatory management and shared financial gains* associated with improved performance, creation of *environmental management systems, operating as a participatory citizen* in the communities in which it operates, and managing all of these mechanisms through *assessment and modifications* based on those they affect.[248]

Collins goes on to note a key theme of this book—that the single most important ethics reference point is an employee's direct manager—how a manager responds to an ethical issue has more influence on employee ethics than any stated policy or direction. This finding aligns well with millennials' desires for ongoing and meaningful communication with their managers. These characteristics of ethical and engaged cultures align, and this is a happy coincidence for corporate leaders who desire long-term success and growth.

Our Findings: An Introduction to What Works

As expected, corporate executives we asked to consider the topic of millennials at work had strong opinions. We surveyed 65 executives from diverse industries, ranging from small companies with 1 employee to large with over 200,000 employees, and with annual revenues of $40,000 to over $35 billion USD.[249] Their insights will be incorporated throughout this chapter, along with additional best practice examples from a variety of companies that are directly addressing millennials at work. In our study, we asked several questions intended to explore perceptions of this cohort of young talent, whether the ascribed characteristics of this cohort resonate with the managers' everyday experiences, whether they have developed best practices to navigate management of millennials or to bridge differences in multigenerational workplaces, and which

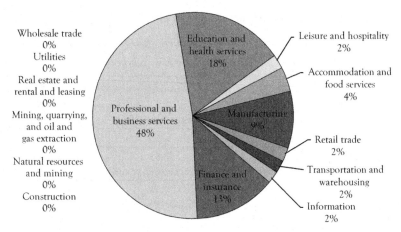

Figure 7.1 Corporate Survey: Industries Represented (n=65)

anecdotes—positive, challenging, or surprising—they could offer. We were glad we asked and we appreciate their candor and insights.

Our findings echoed the research highlights we have explored throughout this book. Managers are occasionally struggling with this young talent—the description "entitled" was offered more than once—but the majority of respondents see tremendous potential and admire their intelligence, skills, and dedication. Among the strongest areas of appreciation for millennial talent are their willingness to work hard when engaged, and their commitment to social and environmental issues. Millennials' penchant for seeking purpose and meaning at work is acknowledged and respected. One executive noted that her approach to managing young talent is guided by "explaining the why behind tasks/ projects that are requested in order to connect to the purpose/mission of our organization." Managers consistently reported awareness that *higher levels of connectedness with millennials leads to increased productivity and organizational outcomes.*

When asked which of the following characteristics often ascribed to millennials resonate with their actual experiences working with young professional, we saw recognition of all of them (Table 7.1).

We can explore several of these items further. First, we can consider the importance of building a connected and engaged culture. As noted in our discussion of mentoring, loyalty is personal rather than to corporation, so

Table 7.1 Characteristics of millennials at work

(Please identify the degree to which you believe these characteristics are repre-sentative of the millennials with whom you have worked (n = 65))

	Strongly agree/Agree	Disagree/ Strongly Disagree
Facility with social media	100%	0%
Technological fluency	96.6% (3.4% neutral/ no opinion)	0%
Awareness of social, environmental, and sustainability issues	79.3% (12.1% neutral/ no opinion)	8.6%
Favor meaningful and fulfilling work	77.6% (12.1% neutral/ no opinion)	10.3%
Proclivity to multitask	56.9% (27.6% neutral/ no opinion)	15.5%
Teamwork capacities	53.4% (29.3% neutral/ no opinion)	17.2%
Preference for training and mentorship (personal attention)	55.1% (27.6% neutral/ no opinion)	17.2%

supervisor and other connections are critical. Creating these connections must be driven by management in an environment where coaching and collaboration are key. How can these connections be developed? To maximize effectiveness, managers can try these approaches:

- *Keep people "in the loop"—communicate explicitly and often. Technology is one example of a mechanism for this communication, and employers do well to make it meaningful and use multiple "voices" (including fostering communication initiated by these young members).*
- *Allow for impact—engage in a way that allows participants to meaningfully contribute—consider our discussion of intrinsic vs. extrinsic motivation in Chapter 5.*
- *Recognize metrics matter—exploring and explicitly discussing outcomes and objectives by answering these types of questions, and not only in financial terms: What have we done? What is our impact? How do we define success as an organization?*

- *Engage around aspirational role models—promote and engage with those who have successfully integrated values and professional life, and who have met the challenges of the specific industry and function of their organizations.*
- *Incorporate mentorship—leader-led and/or peer-to-peer—by explicitly encouraging this professional development opportunity for all employees.*

Research tells us that this works with millennials (and with others!). These approaches align with the *Giving Voice to Values* (GVV) tenants we have considered. One example is the notion of engaging and using *voice* toward values-based decision making and leadership by hosting discussions, engaging online, sharing interesting news, and other approaches, which then aligns with purpose, a proclivity of these young people who were raised with benchmarks and recognition for success, and allow for efficacy and contribution at any organizational level.

Managers are key to the success of these strategies. Corporate leaders must create space for this type of professional development. Dedicating time to discussion of values, and application of and practicing them in real contexts and with colleagues, is necessary for these approaches to be useful. As GVV founder and director Mary Gentile suggests, it is a form of developing "muscle memory." We can build our capacities and instincts to act in alignment with values. Exploring, practicing, and "scripting" effective decision making allow for retrieval and connections among corporate and personal values, and real-world issues. It becomes just another management duty. This values-based decision making is happening at top companies—it is a necessary next iteration of effective business leadership. With explicit attention and development, it is within reach.

Best Practices: Individual Integrity & Organizational Effectiveness

Companies can start with acknowledging a focus on individual integrity. This emphasis recognizes the factors, internally and within the business context, that surround ethical decision making at work. Millennials and their multigenerational coworkers must develop ethical fluency in the organizational and societal contexts to be effective. We start by fostering what scholars call "moral courage"—the courage to make reasoned responses and take deliberative action in the face of challenges. Moral courage is a precursor to contributing to and managing effective, ethical businesses in an era when values questions are answered by our corporate leaders every day.

We also acknowledge the role of contextual factors, which we will discuss next. By understanding how we as individuals develop skills to voice our values, we identify the conditions that make it more likely we will do so, and these "enabling" conditions become a checklist for the type of organizational culture and context of the organizations we lead.[250] Roles and responsibilities of individuals within our organizations shape the culture and expectations. Policies and processes must be structured to incentivize those characteristics and behaviors that allow for success across the triple bottom line of today's organizations—ethical, environmental, and financial performance. Effective organizations must engage around strengthening moral courage and the capacity for internal ethical decision making as foundational.

Many top companies are exploring these issues explicitly. For example, Deloitte, a top professional services firm, works closely with academic partners to explore integrity at work and to distribute and implement these findings on ethical leadership in the corporate world. Key research on cultivating character and developing vibrant, ethical organizations is integrated in collaboration between scholars and practitioners. See http://ethicalleadership.nd.edu for more information.

Tactics toward ethical organizations that are effective with millennials are critical for all employees. Scholars note a general guideline:

The approach that appears to be the most practical and have the greatest potential benefit for the organization as a whole (across all generations) is to treat all employees well. If you provide employees with an interesting job, good compensation, opportunities to learn and advance, colleagues they like to work with, a boss they trust, and leaders who are competent, employees of all generations will respond positively.[251]

By aligning work with purpose and enabling voice, we can successfully enhance management of the organization. Thus, "All employees want to feel valued, empowered, and engaged at work. This is a fundamental need, not a generational issue. And, though Gen Xers and Millennials openly discuss and even demand more flexibility in their jobs, Boomers and Traditionalists (also known as the "Silent Generation") want it too, even if they are less vocal about it." Millennials are driving positive changes. "You can think of the millennials as pushing for change that all generations want to see happen. 'Am I continuing to learn and grow?' is a question that resonates with employees of all ages. The way your organization helps them answer that question may be your competitive advantage in attracting, developing, and keeping tomorrow's talent."[252]

Purpose Revisited

Our discussion in Chapter 5 of exploring personal and professional purpose reminds us to consider *self-knowledge, self-image,* and values *alignment.* Self-awareness is a precursor to values identification and ultimately of ethical judgment and action. Millennials and their managers who explore GVV exercises explore purpose, including personal and professional goals, and self-assess comfort with risk, preferred communication styles, and understandings of loyalty and self-image. One helpful tool, the "Personal-Professional Profile," is included in Appendix B. The information uncovered in the process of self-assessment allows participants to readily frame "levers," or ways of responding, which enable ethical action in a way that is consistent with who they are. Thus, we are all vulnerable to self-justifying biases and ways of viewing our decisions as positively motivated, even when we would criticize another who made similar choices; the task becomes actively considering our personal values, behaviors, and self-image, and aligning them with the kind of person we want to be. We are thus anticipating the choices and "prescripting" our interpretation.[253]

Creating opportunities to engage in this self-reflection, alignment, and "prescripting," or practicing out loud with peers, can be the domain of organizations that value a proactive, strength-building approach to professional development. We will see how several companies have successfully incorporated this and other exercises later in this chapter.

Perhaps the prescripting exercises we incorporate in my class could be useful models for professional development activities in business. Thus, we engage in individual and team role playing exercises using case studies and issues generated by the group to practice ethical decision making and action. In class, these exercises have included scenarios such as the pressure to overbill client hours at an accountancy internship, the dilemma of reneging on a job offer, appropriate expense reporting, plagiarism, among many others, and these are all scenarios derived from the students' own experiences.

Then action must follow intention. After an honest self-reflection and identification of core values, we must operationalize them in our day-to-day decision making—whether we perceive the stakes to be large or small—to mitigate the "slippery slope" or incrementalism of unethical decision making:

> If you give in to "just this once," based on a marginal-cost analysis, you'll regret where you end up. . . . It's easier to hold to your principles 100 percent of the time than it is to hold to them 98 percent of the time. The boundary—your personal moral line—is powerful because you don't cross it; if you have justified doing it once, there's nothing to stop you doing it again. Decide what you stand for. And then stand for it all the time.[254]

This prescripting or deliberate practice of anticipating and developing reactions to ethical challenges may have particular resonance with millennials. The desire for a "feedback loop" of action and reinforcement, often levied as a charge that millennials desire because they were raised receiving trophies "just for showing up," can actually be channeled as a powerful and positive characteristic. Feedback, and anticipating and prescripting challenges, can be part of this communication loop that adds value across the board. Discussing potential and past ethical conflicts together with peers and leaders in which we consider the issues, their inception, their resolution, and what happened along the way, and then imagining alternatives, cultivating other ways of communicating, and practicing approaches and responses model this feedback loop. Engaging in discussion of these issues again strengthens our "muscles" for responding to new challenges. It also opens the door to professional development in a meaningful way.

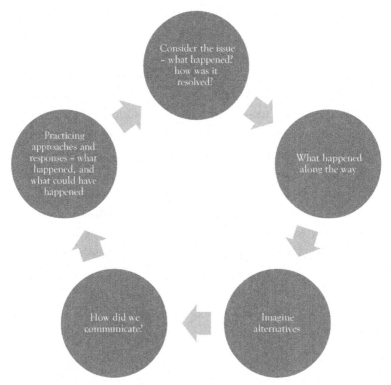

Figure 7.2   Feedback Loop: Discussion of Potential and Past Ethical Conflicts

These feedback loops are critical for millennial development (Figure 7.2). Though millennials have certainly experienced more positive praise, they do understand the difference between recognition contingent on skill and effort, and those noncontingent recognitions for simply "showing up." As one social scientist notes, "Ask . . . kids which of their many trophies are most valuable to them and they point to the ones they earned through skill and effort, not the ones they got for showing up. . . . [Other formative activities in the millennial experience such as video games] also provide this immediate feedback loop, with both positive and negative reinforcement."[255] This research again acknowledges the millennial desire for specific and constructive feedback, and the type of feedback that can help all of us perform optimally:

> [It] turns out what millennials are asking for is what the science of behavior tells us is the best way to manage performance. . . . Millennials want frequent and specific feedback and they don't mind negative feedback if it makes it clear how to improve. They want clear expectations and want to know where they stand relative to those expectations. This is exactly what the science of behavior tells us to do to produce optimum work environments: pinpoint what you want, provide frequent and specific feedback on performance and provide contingent positive reinforcement for progress and accomplishment (ideally linked to impact). Millennials are demanding good management whereas other generations did not.[256]

Once again, management approaches that reflect the best in young talent can enhance organizational outcomes, and can bring out the best in members of every generation.

One simple method of incorporating a feedback loop is using real-time polling programs in workshops or other professional development opportunities at work—available free or at low-cost online. These tools are popular and easy ways to prompt discussion around ethical topics at work. Participants can quickly and anonymously reply to questions with responses displayed on-screen for all participants to react and engage around discussion topics. In my own experiences, when used in the classroom or in executive trainings, the response to these tools has been overwhelmingly positive. They signal and model a communication loop and involve participants explicitly and easily. They set the foundation for discussion of key issues in an inclusive and engaging way.

Setting the Stage for Values Discussions

How to incorporate these topics, and first broach them, is important. The introduction of the GVV course at Notre Dame, a topic I have explored in a previous article,[257] might be usefully analogous to implementing explicit values considerations in a professional setting. GVV has been used successfully by companies around the world and specific exercises are available as noted above; I can speak directly to my own experiences with millennials in the business classroom. The course thus offers a model for implementing similar approaches in professional workshops or trainings.

First, careful consideration of how the course should be marketed to participants was key. We frame the course explicitly as practical, strategic skill development. Less effective would be encouraging students (and likely, employees) to "talk about values." The students receive introductory materials describing this approach to enhancing effective decision making, thus positioning these values conversations as necessary for effective business leadership. The approach is inherently aspirational and appeals to the millennial desire to signal and practice implementable skills.

In class we discuss the importance of principled reasoning in effective decision making and leadership. We acknowledge the necessity of credibility in leading and consensus building, and that effective policy and strategy decisions must be rooted in principle. These emphases are consistent with skills students have expressed as priority for career advancement. In addition to this pragmatic frame, we emphasize the course as an opportunity to give voice, so that students feel inspired to contribute, participate, and lead based on who they are and what they value. These desires are thus validated and channeled into actionable skills—an approach that is likely to be successful with millennials in the workplace.

The manager's role can also include prompting alignment between personal values and those of the corporation. Here, as we have explored earlier, we can recognize the necessarily broad definition of corporate purpose. To echo our discussion in Chapter 5 we can consider a much-shared TED talk, in which Unilever COO Harish Manwani notes that "profit is not always the point," describing Unilever's forays into dedicated community impact projects and other mechanisms to create social value as critical for those companies that will thrive in the modern era. Manwani describes the new paradigm as incorporating a fourth "G" in the traditional conception of the three G's of growth: growth that is consistent, growth that is competitive, and growth that is profitable—this fourth "G" must involve growth that is responsible. Thus, we "need businesses that can actually define their role in society in terms of a much larger purpose than the products and brands they sell."[258] Ethical conduct will be a competitive advantage in this era in which the stakes are so high. Millennials, who indicate the importance of the character of their work time and again in a growing body of research, are poised to contribute significantly within this space.

A few additional notes on the academic course in GVV that may be useful for business leaders considering adoption of these approaches in their own companies:

(1) *Build on the strengths of your organization—incorporate stories and cases from your industry, and your people, and explicitly consider organizational values.*

(2) *Make it relevant—use current examples and encourage participants to contribute their own. Allow these young professionals, and all members of your organization, to motivate and learn from one another. As one of my students noted, "The insights from my fellow students have been the most rewarding part of this class. I have been really impressed."*[259]

(3) *Use what is available—the GVV collection (largely open-source, with permission) features foundational readings, cases, and teaching notes— the tools are readily accessible.*

We have explored some of the tips provided by students studying millennial management toward ethical organizations; I also asked these millennials to include their own tips for leaders to manage possible resistance from employees who are involved in implementing these types of new processes. Several suggestions include:

- *One resistance might be employees thinking "I don't want to be a mentor." Some employees will be better suited to mentor a new hire than others. However, it is important that all employees try this relationship from both sides at least once as it can serve as a valuable leadership experience. Employees could be made aware of this duty once the program is implemented and then upon each new employee's start with the company. Feedback from both the mentor and mentee could be collected to see how the mentee is progressing and to see if the mentor is suited to continue in this role and possibly do it again in the future.*

- *Managers might hear "I don't need ethics training." Ethics training will be mandatory for all members of the company. By making it a company-wide endeavor—including high-ranking executives—it should help counter resistance.*
- *One method by which we could manage the possibility of senior executives resisting the new changes would be to make sure that they are involved in the process of implementing the changes. The two key factors to getting everybody on board with the new program is to clearly show the facts that support the decision and by bringing a sense of ownership and involvement in the program. First, it will be important to present facts that show that the proposed changes will be successful in attracting top talent and in creating value for the firm. The department in charge of hiring should put together a presentation to be held live for the managers in the firm. The presentation should consist of several clearly articulated facts from business journals, academic studies, or industry data, concerning what millennials desire when they seek work. The managers will understand that the firm must continuously hire top talent for future success and so the presentation could show the managers how to attract this top talent. The specific components of the program should be discussed in detail and show that the proposed changes will lead to a better environment for all employees.*
- *A tangible recommendation to address any anticipated friction is to have a short webinar that summarizes both the generation differences data, and the specific reasons for implementing the program itself. (MM students)*

A top U.S. insurance provider shared this strategy for a workshop around ethics and values that was designed for leaders but has become so successful that it is now instituted throughout the organization:

From our company archives of employee bad or questionable behavior we created a series of case cards. Teams of 5 to 7 leaders or employees work together to discuss the case issues, make decisions, and specify the best course of ethical leadership action. We ask them to use whatever resources they think would assist, [for example] our Code of Ethics, company policies, company values, or other resources. After discussing the cases provided, folks are asked to write up a real case [based on a] situation they observed— but to leave out any traceable details. Cases are placed in a pile and one by one a member of the groups picks one up and leads the discussion. The workshop was designed to be 90 minutes, but often runs longer as folks seem to want to continue discussing the situations. We save the newly written cases and turn them into preprinted cards to be used with other groups. We've found this design works with all age groups and often the bigger the age spread the more lively the conversation.[260]

The academic and corporate contexts offer other areas of overlap. When it comes to cultivating desired behavior, perhaps not surprisingly, research indicates that the same psychological processes, rationalizations, and reasons are cited both by students engaged in academic dishonesty, and by corporate executives observing wrongdoing.[261] In a study of more than 300 CEOs in firms with annual revenues of $10 million or more, both publicly and privately owned, when asked, "How important are these factors for explaining unethical conduct in most organizations?", CEOs reported the following results, ranked high to low[262]:

- personal greed;
- failure of the organization's leadership in establishing ethical standards and culture;
- weakness of personal character;
- desire to advanced career;
- pressure to meet unrealistic performance or financial goals;
- indifference or low morale;
- pressure to meet deadlines and schedules;
- failure of the organization to establish an effective compliance;
- desire to harm the employer;
- not understanding the company's ethics policies;
- not agreeing with the company's ethics policies.

Again, these are listed in order of the perception of their importance, and it is important to note that CEOs ranked all of these factors as "important." We could deconstruct each of these, and it is easy to see how exploring the GVV pillars of voice, normality, purpose, self-assessment and alignment, reasons and rationalizations and values are illuminating as resources to address these. We can also see both personal and organizational dynamics reflected, pointing toward an approach to building ethical companies that include both aspects.

Executives also express that these dynamics are concerns regardless of level within the company—they are contextual for millennials and new hires, and their managers. Short-term thinking, unrealistic time and performance pressures absent other evaluation and development measures, high stakes without anticipating responses. . . . These are traps that we can, and companies do, manage. A useful step is to examine personal and organizational barriers to ethical action.

Barriers to Ethical Action

Many of the barriers that can challenge our attempts to fulfill our individual and organizational purpose are described in the GVV curriculum as "reasons and rationalizations." They can manifest as objections from colleagues when one tries to voice an ethical concern, or can be the unspoken assumptions that exist in the workplace. Taking the time to anticipate and create responses to the most typical reasons and rationalizations that we will confront in our workplaces is key to successfully managing them. This can be another consideration in the design of managerial policies and approaches, and can serve as material for exploration in professional development activities. As discussed previously, the very act of "normalizing" ethical challenges at work helps create a space for consideration of these issues in a direct and thoughtful way. Millennial penchant for direct and collaborative engagement around these topics provides a helpful foundation for exploring them at work.

Considering those values conflicts that occur most frequently in our particular industry or job function can also be helpful. Accountants face different dilemmas than sales professionals. The act of familiarizing ourselves, and those we manage, with the types of values conflicts that are common in our area of work normalizes and helps prepare us for managing them. In the aspirational spirit of our approach, we suggest exploring the outcomes of different choices, and specifically including examples of individuals who have successfully voiced and acted on their values in that specific situation. These "case studies" can be quite powerful. The GVV collection provides many of these, at no charge to the users, by functional area (i.e., accountancy, marketing, finance). Through individual and role-playing exercises, participants practice ethical decision making and action.

But such cases can be found internally as well. These examples from within are accessible and instructive. Bringing these to the table for discussion can be powerful and persuasive. Research finds that exposure to positive role models have significant benefits in the development of students studying business by "protecting against reduced self-efficacy by showing that unethical behavior is neither necessary nor inevitable in business, thus undermining the common justification for unethical behavior that 'everybody does it'. . . . Positive role models increase awareness that business can be both ethical and profitable."[263] Case examples that focus on positive resolutions rather than "what not to do" appeal to millennial efficacy reduce cynicism and open the door to creative and impactful resolutions to challenges at work.

Another categorization of values conflicts includes considering the types of arguments or rationalizations. These most common types of arguments, illustrated in the GVV research, include[264]:

- Expected or Standard Practice: "Everyone does this, so it's really standard practice. It's even expected."
- Materiality: "The impact of this action is not material. It doesn't really hurt anyone."
- Locus of Responsibility: "This is not my responsibility; I'm just following orders here."
- Locus of Loyalty: "I know this isn't quite fair to the customer but I don't want to hurt my reports/team/boss/company."

We can become adept at responding to each of these as we become familiar with them. Thus, for example, an appeal to "standard practice" is often exaggeration—if everyone were actually doing "it" (whatever the "it" may be in a particular situation), and if the practice is really accepted, why are there typically laws, rules, and policies against it? What would be the consequences for consumer trust and business practice if everyone did "it"? Would we be comfortable if everyone knew we were doing "it"? These and other questions help us consider whether this argument is truly persuasive. More discussion on these "reasons and rationalizations" is provided in the GVV collection; for our purposes it is key to acknowledge that these types of arguments are often employed, and there are strategies that can enable us to be more successful in responding to them.

How might we respond to these reasons and rationalizations? Just as there are patterns of arguments rationalizing ethically questionable behavior, there are corresponding ways of responding to them, or levers, that can be helpful. These levers include recognizing and unpacking false dichotomies (for example, the very reasonable aversion to putting ourselves at a disadvantage at work can be used to justify all sorts of ethically questionable behavior, if we frame the choice as one between ethical action that results in personal or organizational consequences, and unethical behavior that leads to some "good" for the self or organization). Other levers identified in the GVV approach[265] include:

- thinking in the long term as well as the short term;
- considering the situation in terms of the organization's wider purpose (are we here to make the monthly numbers, or to create a vibrant and sustainable organization for our stakeholders?);
- confronting a narrow view of managerial purpose by reconsidering the definition of "competitive advantage" toward overall and long-term excellence as opposed to merely beating the competition—this has implications for *how* we achieve results, in addition to determining whether we achieve them;
- positioning oneself as an agent of "continuous improvement" rather than as the source of complaint;
- positioning oneself as a source of actionable alternatives rather than "thou shalt nots";

- addressing addictive cycles that can cause increasing risks and pressures that lead to greater and greater values conflicts;
- exploring who we need and can attract as an ally in our efforts;
- considering the costs to each affected party—what is at stake for those affected, and how can we recognize and mitigate these risks to make our arguments more appealing;
- assuming that our audience is made up of pragmatists—not idealists or opportunists—but generally good people who want to do the "right thing" without feeling as though they have been exploited for doing so, or that they will be at a systematic disadvantage if they do so;
- countering the commonly held assumption that most pragmatists expect—that of the lowest common denominator of behavior by those around them—by motivating individuals to step beyond this lowest common denominator by sharing examples of effective managers who have made ethical choices.

These levers can be particularly effective for millennials and their managers as they align nicely with the characteristics and preferences of action-oriented young professionals that desire a continuous and open feedback loop on performance and impact. When we acknowledge and explore these, we equip ourselves to readily recognize them, to understand the ways of thinking that produce them, and to be assured and practiced in responding to them.

A Culture of Integrity

As we work toward effective, ethical organizations, we can build on the foundation of personal integrity and consider culture at work. We must consider organizational effectiveness, or the systems and processes put in place to foster decision making in accordance with corporate values. A first step can be acknowledging the role of what scholars call moral imagination. We often ask ourselves "what should be done?" when facing a difficult ethical challenge—both as individuals, and within organizations as managerial conduct is framed in terms of "should." Moral imagination recognizes the benefit of unconventional thinking and innovative problem-solving—a proclivity that can align well with the skills of talented millennials. Thus, "shifting one's mindset from 'What should I do?' to 'What could I do?' generates moral insight, defined as the realization that ostensibly competing values are not entirely incompatible. Moral insight allows for exploration of more possible solutions beyond the apparent constraints of the problem provided, and for the formulation of creative solutions that satisfy multiple moral imperatives."[266]

This "could" mindset opens a broad range of possibilities: "Employees and teams might devise practical solutions that resolve the inherent tension in a dilemma. Rather than assume a fixed contest that requires adjudication and a tradeoff, . . . with some unconventional thinking, managers can generate solutions to ethical dilemmas."[267] Brainstorming and identifying these ideas of what "could" happen can be done in collaboration with others to create stronger teams and more cohesive organizations that acknowledge the contributions of all.

Other best practices in creating ethical cultures and managing millennials align well with the GVV tenets of encouraging voice, normalizing values discussions, engaging in peer coaching, defining purpose explicitly and broadly, and allowing for self-assessment and alignment. A report on "Maximizing Millennials in the Workplace" produced by the University of North Carolina's Kenan-Flagler Business School[268] includes several tips, many explored in other areas of this book, which relate specifically to creating ethical, effective cultures. These include communicating to prospective employees what the business does to engage employees, including doing so through technological tools such as recruiting websites, and developing activities that foster support and understanding among the generations, including explicit training on intergenerational dynamics—for example, for millennials, offering soft-skills training on assimilating to new workplace cultures, how to work effectively, assertively, and diplomatically, how to process feedback, how to approach a supervisor for coaching, and how to set long-term career goals.

Other tips in the Kenan-Flagler report include offering collaborative discussions, fostering an appreciation for diversity, encouraging open communication, considering reverse mentoring and other innovative

approaches, offering learning opportunities such as tuition reimburse-
ment or funds for professional development, which increase retention
rates and appeal to millennial goals of continuous learning, and levering
technology and teamwork. These strategies reinforce shared values and
expectations for ethical decision making.[269] Here we can again visit some
suggestions from millennial students studying effective management of
young talent toward ethical, effective leadership:

*While these generations differ greatly in their values and attitudes, their dif-
ferences may be utilized as a business advantage for companies in the form of
cross-generational teams. Cross-generational teams will be central to success in
the future, as diverse groups will be better prepared to handle diverse client
bases. With employee members from different backgrounds and ages, teams
will be much more effective at problem solving and creating solutions because
they will be better able to frame issues through multiple lenses; in effect, teamwork capacity will increase. (MM student)*

How can managers and other leaders cultivate integrity and actively
discourage unethical behavior? Cressey's classic discussion of the "fraud
triangle" of pressure, perceived opportunity, and rationalization merits a quick mention here. These three conditions are typically present
when fraud occurs at work—again acknowledging that most employee
wrongdoing is not the province of "evil." Certainly "bad apples" exist,
but we can recall our early discussion of the "bell curve," with most of
us operating in the category of pragmatists who would like to do the
right thing as long as it does not put us at a systematic disadvantage.
Robust ethics and compliance programs, including efforts in hiring,
supervising, and promotion, seem to be our best foil for mitigating the
damaging effects of those who will pursue self-interest regardless of cost
to others.

Our opportunity for cultivating ethical cultures lies with the majority of our employees. Most unethical behavior at work is committed by
trusted employees with no history of wrong doing. Often otherwise de-
cent people rationalize and engage in "slippery slope" behavior in the
context of organizational conditions. This does not mean, of course, that

unethical employees are the fault of their employer. Rather, leaders can and should create conditions that acknowledge this dynamic, and foster ethical cultures where wrongdoing is not a ready alternative. Leaders must acknowledge the very real and important role they have in cultivating the desired ethos of their organization.

As discussed in Chapter 3, Lang (2013) provides a well-researched list of learning environments that induce cheating. While Lang's work focuses on the academic context, I contend that these ideas are transferable. In the classroom or in the boardroom, instructors and managers can minimize the contextual factors that actually enhance the possibility of unethical behavior. This list of "what *not* to do"[270] includes structuring organizations and processes such that:

- motivation is extrinsic, only or primarily;
- orientation toward performance is supreme;
- infrequent, high-stakes assessments are the means for measuring performance;
- students (employees) feel low self-efficacy;
- cheating is perceived as common and approved by peers.

We have discussed the extrinsic motivation factor in Chapter 5, and its particular dissonance with millennial desires. When young people experience motivation that is external (money, status) *absent* internal motivation such as feelings of accomplishment, satisfaction, and contribution, they are not only unhappier, they are more likely to engage in unethical behavior to achieve those extrinsic rewards. Doing a job well, for the sake of those intrinsic motivations, must be part of the package.

Similarly, performance goals and assessments that exist absent notions of development, reciprocity, engagement, and contribution toward shared goals with a focus on broad notions of professional purpose are problematic. They clearly run the risk of inducing members to take shortcuts to achieve those metrics without embracing the spirit behind them and the long-term implications for organizational and personal success. We need only look at the myriad examples of executive compensation tied solely to stock value (Enron, anyone?) or commission incentives absent other measures of performance (a key factor in the subprime mortgage crisis) to witness how readily these type of incentive and evaluation systems can foster unethical means of achieving these goals.

Again this is not to excuse individual unethical behavior. We all have a choice. Yet context and conditions matter. Our approach suggests that we are all more likely to be successful in acting consistently with our values, and with the values of the organization as a whole, when we operate within systems that acknowledge human dynamics, and maximize the potential for ethical decision making and leadership.

Efficacy is another key area of attention. As discussed, millennials appreciate and are inclined toward feelings of effectiveness, contribution, engagement, and being valued. Managers must create systems that promote self-efficacy—by involving employees in decision making, cultivating open and consistent dialogue, promoting transparency about process, and including explicit discussion of how each part contributes to the whole. These are required elements for millennial contribution, and have the additional benefit of enhancing the ethical climate for all employees. We are less likely to behave unethically if we feel we are acknowledge and connected. A culture that encourages voice and dialogue is one less susceptible to disastrous consequences of a lack of transparency. For just one example, in the wake of its massive automobile recall, we are learning now about the voices of dissent that were effectively silenced at General Motors—a culture that appeared to respond indifferently or, at worst, actively discourage speaking up, in the face of very real safety concerns.[271]

Finally, the tenor of the peer culture is critical for millennial success. Millennials are motivated by and motivate one another, and they communicate about these connections constantly. Engaging young leaders to help express corporate values is critical. We all have mission and values statements. We need to think about how they are displayed, discussed, understood, exemplified, and reinforced. Research indicates that universities and colleges with expressed honor codes are much less likely to experience episodes of academic dishonesty.[272] Perhaps surprisingly, less than 25 percent of U.S. universities incorporate a formal honor code,[273] which is an untapped area of opportunity to "name" and "normalize" ethical considerations at the organizational level.

The first step is to identify and communicate these values. Yet, again, all we need to do is look at Enron's lengthy and eloquent code of ethics and values to see that the conversation must extend beyond such statements. As corporate comic hero Dilbert asks his boss: "Can you explain how the company's new 'Statement of Core Values' will change my behavior? I was planning to poison the town's water supply. But wait! It's against our core values!"[274] Creating a culture of integrity is key—a clear feedback loop must be established so expectations are clear and reinforced, and the rules are enforced and violations addressed, consistently and transparently.[275] When assessing values at work, specific behaviors must be explored—rather than sweeping statements such as "do you act with integrity?", managers can facilitate discussion around specific actions, such as "how often do you (complete tasks on time, return e-mails, and so on)?" Again the connections among employees and with managers is also key; as one millennial remarked, *"It's not so much the COMPANY values that are important (anyone can say something on a sheet of paper) . . . it is the PEOPLE/PEERS at the company who I want my values to match."*

Harvard researchers have explored the two broad approaches to mitigating unethical behavior at work, namely *"values-oriented approaches* that broadly appeal to individuals' preferences to be more moral" and *"structure-oriented approaches* that redesign specific incentives, tasks and decisions to reduce temptations to cheat in the environment," and they conclude that integration of *both* approaches, while avoiding incompatible strategies, can reduce the risk of adverse effects of only employing a single approach.[276] Peer and aspirational leader reinforcement is a promising approach for millennials and all employees, and is another illustration of the central GVV pillars of values and purpose, voice, and normality. A conversation about the *how* and the *why* of expressed corporate values must not start and end at employee onboarding. It is not enough to set expectations—they must be reinforced. The act of frequent retrieval of these values and expectations—with examples, and ideally in collaboration with others—develops our capacity to understand and apply them.

Managing Millennials: Recruiting and Onboarding

There are many opportunities to develop the leadership capacity of millennials toward organizational goals and this process largely begins at our business schools. Our task at b-schools is to prime emerging leaders with competencies and inclinations toward effective, ethical business leadership. We must provide opportunities to learn and practice key competencies and critical analyses, and we must normalize ethical considerations so that they are best equipped to recognize and manage them in the workplace. By providing engagement and interaction around ethical decision models, exploration of best practices from the field, and opportunities to practice and apply these principles, business schools can set the stage for success in professional careers. This foundation helps prime emerging professionals as they seek employment that aligns with their goals.

Students are increasingly considering values issues during the employment search, with explicit attention to corporate ethics during the research and interview process. At the same time, employers, mindful of the context of today's business, are seeking new hires that can "do well" and "do good." Research indicates that too few companies ask ethics-related questions in interviews, an approach that can benefit the company in many ways. For example, companies may ask candidates to describe an example of an ethical challenge they have faced, and how they addressed it. These types of questions are intended less to identify individuals of strong character than to convey that ethics matters in important ways. This benefits both the candidate and the interviewer: "It can be helpful to reinforce in compliance training for managers the importance of ethics-related job interviewing—as this helps convey the larger message that managers are responsible for the conduct of those who report to them."[277]

A helpful tool for both employer and candidate during the interview process is the *Ethical Recruiting Practices Guide*[278] provided here. The guide includes helpful tips including explicit discussion of ethical considerations that are aligned with the GVV principles of normalizing and voicing values as a critical component.

Managers could also consider incorporating variations on this approach, suggested by students studying effective millennial management:

Management can incorporate a "Group Challenge" as part of the interview process for new hires. The "group challenge" would be a teamwork-centered event in which candidates work together. Interviewers will observe the interactions, and may choose to discuss what they see in the group interview that follows. The group interview will allow the interviewers and interviewee time to ask any final questions or address observations from the team exercise (MM student).

ETHICS & INTEGRITY IN BUSINESS
IMPORTANCE FOR THE RECRUITING PROCESS
Second Edition

JOB APPLICANTS
(guide for companies and recruiters on reverse)

Benefits of Working for an Ethical Employer:

- Ethical companies treat employees fairly and with respect.
- These organizations create an environment where employees aren't pressured to compromise company standards or their personal values.
- They often provide training and guidance to assist employees in making ethical decisions.
- Firms with proven reputations for highly-ethical behavior attract other principled, qualified employees—this self-selection creates a reinforcing "norm."

Practices Job Seekers Should AVOID:

- Misrepresenting one's background or skills in interviews or on a resume.
- Accepting on-site interviews when they are unlikely to accept an offer from the prospective employer.
  - Misrepresenting job seeking status (e.g., number of offers).
  - Exhibiting unprofessional behavior (e.g., making disparaging comments, fraternizing with recruiters, or posting personal or inappropriate information on social media platforms).
  - Reneging on an acceptance of a job offer—either ask for an extension or say no.

FACT: The 2011 Corporate Recruiters Survey* asked 1,509 employers in 51 countries what primary traits and abilities they sought in MBA candidates. INTEGRITY ranked in the top three of 18 identified attributes, along with professionalism and initiative.

Questions You Might Ask Companies and Recruiters:**

- Is there a formal statement of ethics (whether a code, values statement, or credo)? How is it distributed, reinforced, and "lived" by the organization?
- Are employees at all levels trained in ethical decision making? Is ethics an integral part of leadership development programs?
- Do employees have multiple channels available to express their concerns confidentially and without fear of retaliation? How does leadership encourage pushback and "getting bad news early?"
- How does top management set the tone regarding ethics and values?
- What types of community service are available? Is participating in service a part of the organization's culture?

ERC
ETHICS
RESOURCE
CENTER

Notre Dame Deloitte
Center for Ethical Leadership

UNIVERSITY OF
NOTRE DAME
Mendoza College of Business
Professor Patrick E. Murphy, Ph.D.

* Conducted by the Graduate Management Admission Council in cooperation with the MBA Career Services Council and the European Foundation for Management Development.
** Adapted from Trevino, L. K. & Nelson, K. Managing Business Ethics: Straight Talk About How To Do It Right. 5th ed. NY: John Wiley & Sons, Inc. 2011. Answers to some of these questions can be found on organizations' websites. Only pick a few to ask during interviews.

Figure 7.1 Ethical recruiting guide

Murphy, Patrick E. 2013 "Ethics and Integrity in Business: Importance for the Recruiting Process" 2nd Edition, available at http://ethicalleadership.nd.edu/assets/110978/ethical_recruiting_practices_guide_2ed_.pdf.

ETHICS & INTEGRITY IN BUSINESS
IMPORTANCE FOR THE RECRUITING PROCESS
Second Edition

**COMPANIES &
RECRUITERS**
(guide for job
applicants on reverse)

Benefits of Hiring an Ethical Employee:

▶ Ethical employees are ambassadors for the company, reinforcing a values-driven culture.

▶ They safeguard the organization's reputation, saving it from costly regulatory violations and loss of revenue through fraud and abuse of resources.

▶ Such individuals demonstrate higher levels of employee commitment and engagement.

▶ They have a broader sense of responsibility and can be trusted to exercise good judgment in challenging situations.

Ethics Questions Recruiters Should Consider Asking Job Applicants:

▶ Describe an ethical dilemma you have faced as a student or employee. How did you identify it, and what steps did you take to resolve it?

▶ Tell me about a time when your integrity was tested.

▶ What does "business ethics" mean to you?

▶ Who would you first consult if faced with a workplace or personal ethical issue?

▶ What personal values guide you in making ethical decisions in your life?

Recruiters Should AVOID:

FACT:

The 2012 Global Management Education Graduate Survey* asked 6,292 graduate management students at 130 business schools worldwide to rate the importance of 25 attributes or selection criteria related to the jobs and companies they were considering. One of the highest was corporate culture, defined by "high ethical standards, emphasis on community and inclusion, fit with organizational culture and organizational climate."

▶ Withholding or misrepresenting relevant information in extending a job offer (e.g., salary, relocation allowance, start date, job title, etc.).

▶ Glorifying or exaggerating job responsibilities or inaccurately portraying the growth potential of a position within the company.

▶ Exhibiting unprofessional behavior (e.g., fraternizing with applicants, harassing them, or making inappropriate connections via social media).

▶ Revoking a job offer or placing unrealistic deadlines or pressure on candidates to make a decision.

▶ Tying a signing bonus to an exploding job offer (e.g., failing to allow applicants to participate in the entire recruiting season, or giving applicants less than two weeks to decide on an offer).

▶ Using high pressure interviewing tactics on campus or during site visits.

Notre Dame Deloitte
Center for Ethical Leadership

**UNIVERSITY OF
NOTRE DAME**
Mendoza College of Business
Professor Patrick E. Murphy, Ph.D.

ERC
ETHICS
RESOURCE
CENTER

* The Global Management Education Graduate Survey is a product of the Graduate Management Admission Council (GMAC), a global nonprofit education organization of leading graduate business schools.

Figure 7.1 Continued

Another student suggests:

All applicants who are deemed to have the technical skills need for the job would be interviewed for open positions. The first round of interviews is set up to accommodate many interviewees at the same time. The first interview will have three interviewees and two interviewers. One interviewer will be a senior executive. The other will be an employee in the middle of the company's hierarchy. The goal is to simulate the actual workplace where different types of employees, from different generations and backgrounds, interact and work together. Specifically, interviewers should see if they are able to lead the discussion effectively when needed and if they can step back and facilitate when needed. Candidates who thrive in the first interview are set up with a one-on-one interview later. This interview allows the employee to get to know the candidate on an individual level to get a better idea if they would fit in the company's plans and philosophy (MM student).

Managing Millennials: Culture at Work

Though we toss the word around frequently, how many of us have given explicit attention to defining and shaping the "culture" of our workplaces? The Harvard Business Review blog ran a piece on elements of a great culture—vision, values, practices, people, narrative, and place[279]— and embedded in each of these are GVV principles. Identifying and integrating vision and values, reinforcing through processes, investing in recruiting and retention policies that align with the other elements beyond simple skill identification, and dedicating voice and space to telling your organization's story and cultivating it by recognizing that these shared stories shape the culture every day. It has been said often, but its truth remains—culture trumps strategy, every time.

These principles are as relevant for small companies as for large. A "thoughtful approach to culture" characterized the winners of Inc. Magazine's "Top Small Companies" designation (to qualify, companies must be privately held, with no more than 500 employees). These leaders embody several key characteristics, including fairly, and often generously, treating workers, respecting work–life balance, and endowing work with meaning. "In return, those employees bestow their best ideas and efforts on the business. They pull together through change and hard times. But the Top Small Company Workplaces are not just 'nice' in a generic way. The leaders of these companies do not try to be all things to all people. Rather, they want to create the best possible workplaces for the kinds of people who can help them succeed."[280] Embedded in each of these approaches is treating employees with dignity and cultivating integrity.

Research on systems that organizations put in place to promote ethical behavior by employees indicates that the *roles* of employees within the organization have implications for their responsiveness to these approaches, clearly a concern for millennials and their managers.[281] Thus, Pitesa and Thau (2013) found that those occupying powerful organizational roles will be least likely to respond to social influence-based systems, which range from explicit organizational ethical standards to others' behavior as an indirect indicator of acceptable conduct in their organization, and may need more incentives (both "carrots" and "sticks") to pay attention to these systems than do those lacking power.

Further, organizations will have particular difficulty fostering ethical conduct among powerful organizational members if these members possess unethical preferences—a finding that underscores the importance of selecting those people with values consistent with the organization's mission for positions of leadership.

Additionally, these scholars found that employees lacking power (such as young talent and new hires) might be particularly vulnerable to unethical social influence, an effect that may be mitigated by efforts to promote employees' abilities to call to mind their personal standards when confronted with a moral issue, through such techniques as practicing "if-then" scenarios, or *prescripting* in the language of GVV, to strengthen their abilities to focus on personal standards of ethical behavior when facing a moral challenge at work.[282]

Managing Millennials: Troubleshooting

How should corporations think about violations of company policies and resulting consequences? What is the goal of this correction—to punish? To rehabilitate? To express corporate values and expectations to the organization (whose members are, of course, watching how infractions are addressed)? As an example of reinforcing expectations around values, one university involved students in a marketing class designing a communication strategy for the university to invigorate understanding around academic integrity policies. It became a way for students to emphasize community norms. It involved ownership by these young leaders. It resulted in enhanced awareness of expectations and policies in a way that sending out a mailing from the president may not. Similarly, corporate values discussions that consist of a mailing and an electronic confirmation of receipt—an all-too frequent strategy—are insufficient. Multigenerational teams engaging with the mission—through discussions, interactive activities, and peer-to-peer examples—create impact in a real and meaningful way.

One more important consideration: as companies work to design effective recruitment and retention strategies, the transparency inherent with the internet ups the ante. Candidates and employees are well aware of those companies identified as "best to work for," and of policies and practices of individual companies. More discussion of this dynamic is provided in Chapter 2.

Managing Millennials: Training and Development

Perhaps not surprisingly, research tells us that despite the sometimes new and challenging characteristics of millennials, we have tremendous potential for impact—the *methods of training and engagement* matter when considering what works! How can corporations create the contexts to engage young professionals toward organizational goals? How can millennials leverage their strengths and manage their challenges toward effective, impactful contribution? We have explored many suggestions so far. We can look to some specific corporate examples for illustration. Most reflect a shared role for millennials and their managers. As just one example, consider the response from a partner at a major professional services firm when asked about millennials and their preference for work–life balance (cited as the most desired characteristics by their new hires): the passion in her voice was palpable as she noted, "They can have it, but they have to earn it first!"

Companies and their young talent can come together to maximize millennial effectiveness toward individual and organizational goals. Best practice examples abound (as do vivid examples of what-not-to-do), and more are emerging every day as this population joins the ranks of business in unprecedented numbers. In addition to our own corporate survey, we scanned the literature for highlights that illustrate promising approaches. Best practices here come from our research and from that of others exploring managing millennials. We highlight strategies of just a few here, with some companies explicitly incorporating explicit GVV approaches, and others using techniques that align with our GVV pillars, both of which effectively develop millennial capacities toward organizational goals.

Corporate Examples

Global consulting firm **McKinsey & Company** has incorporated the GVV curriculum into training since 2012, and its efforts are illustrative for other firms. McKinsey notes that the GVV approach aligns well with its global mission in several key ways that reflect its resonance for managing talent in today's workplaces. A profile on their incorporation of GVV notes appreciation for the GVV approach as one that aligns with a strength-based approach to leadership development, and recognizes the importance of dialogue, including acknowledging that "open discussion among caring but dissenting colleagues as critical to preserving [the firm's] values."[283] Other key features of McKinsey's approach also reflect their incorporation of GVV: "In working with [the approach, our managers] realized that moving from awareness to action on values requires changes in specific skills, not just belief. Building the 'muscle' to speak up for our values requires dedicated attention by individuals and their organizations."[284]

McKinsey also incorporates a dedicated global Values Day that includes scripting exercises based on GVV that includes role-play scenarios and development of action plans for responding to ethical challenges. Participants also draft a set of sample phrases to use when raising a values issue (for example, "Help me understand what you meant when. . . .") and other prompts for encouraging dialogue. Ninety-seven percent of participating employees felt that they were "able to engage in honest, authentic dialogue about our values" through the exercise.[285] This is an approach that will clearly resonate with millennials, who want to work with colleagues across the organization, to feel that they are involved and connected, and to witness aspirational role models and their peers explicitly engaging around values.

McKinsey also dedicates attention to the approach for both senior partners and new managers. Using GVV content, their leadership development team created a session for senior partners during an orientation training for newly elected senior shareholders: "During the session, the Directors reflected on the specific enablers that have allowed them to speak up for their values in the past. Then they discussed how they could ensure those enablers are present in their teams—to support more junior colleagues in voicing their values."[286] The session is well received with participants noting an appreciation for the practical nature and helpful reinforcement of serving as senior role models. McKinsey incorporates this approach for others in the organization as well:

> Upon promotion to the role of manager, consultants at the firm participate in an off-site training in which they rehearse a challenging conversation that they would like to initiate, or have recently experienced, with a client or colleague. This GVV session underscores several themes. First, to develop peer-like relationships with clients and McKinsey's senior leaders, managers must give voice to both Firm and personal values. Second, to increase their confidence and effectiveness in such conversations, managers must practice. Third, to inspire and motivate the junior consultants whom they now manage, these new managers must demonstrate a willingness themselves to speak up.[287]

In this way, McKinsey is modeling intergenerational mentoring and connection, which is an effective approach for millennials.

General Electric engaged their employees around integrating millennials into its culture by creating a team of millennials from various GE functions and businesses to work with HR on ways to attract, develop, and retain millennial talent. Their three-month assignment resulted in recommendations that have now been adopted by senior leaders—these include using gaming technology to connect the world to GE, and to educate prospective employees about the company's values, creating a personalized suite of flexible benefits that better meets the needs of GE's global, diverse workforce, and enhancing performance management systems with new tools to help employees navigate their careers, identify opportunities throughout the company, and to offer more immediate feedback and coaching.[288] GE also features BuildOn Inc., an outreach effort building schools in impoverished parts of the world, about which CFO Jeff Bornstein remarks, "[these giving programs have] completely changed [employee] perspectives about our company," and who describes BuildOn as a key recruiting tool for new employees.[289]

Design and innovation firm **IDEO**, whose clients have included Apple, Proctor & Gamble, Microsoft, PepsiCo, Ford, and Eli Lilly, argues for a human-centered approach to design called "design empathy," an approach that draws upon people's real-world experiences and awareness of and sensitivity to the perspectives of others that allows designers to develop concepts, services, products, strategies, and systems that are innovative and responsive to real needs and desires.[290] This approach is even more salient in today's global, diverse work environment that requires broad recognition of stakeholders and our interconnectedness with one another and with our social and natural environment. We heard this appreciation for millennials' experience and ease with working in diverse environments repeatedly from our own corporate survey participants.

One IDEO project illustrates the potential for engaging with millennials as employees and as consumers: "State Farm engaged IDEO to help it understand how to make its offerings more relevant to millennials. . . . The first round of research revealed that in addition to not relying on banks and insurance companies as much as previous generations, many young people felt intimidated by them and struggled to find trustworthy financial advice."

The design team developed a solution to this challenge, envisioning an experience for millennials that would respect their concerns and fulfill their need for connection and learning. The result was what they call a "living empathy lab," Next Door, located in Lincoln Park, Chicago—a lively neighborhood filled with young professionals where they provide free, live coaching (but charge for coffee). "For State Farm, it is a valuable experiment that teaches the company how to better deliver on its brand promise of being 'a good neighbor' to a whole new generation. State Farm's bold move underscores that . . . we must help companies create ways to have real relationships with their existing customers and users, as well as with potential customers and users. Empathy enables leadership to have a clear vision for these relationships and develop a strategy for influencing how they ultimately play out."[291]

Explicit attention to social media is a great way to engage millennials, as is employee-driven community activism. Some companies do both simultaneously. Several firms embrace corporate social engagement through social media using a new tool called Neighbourly, which matches corporate giving to community needs. **Starbucks** and **Marks & Spencer** are among the first participants. This method allows for mission alignment and local connections. These types of connections to social causes can and should be motivated by employee interests and enthusiasm. These initiatives allow for employee engagement in new and exciting ways, and enhance the impact of community outreach and commitment.

American Express offers its OPEN online communication forum to explore millennial talents and interests and engages business owners and young professionals in discussion on key topics and best practices. This advice-sharing tool is driven by participants and allows for interconnectedness around shared interests.

We can also consider several other corporate examples of engaged employees, and the specific connections with ethical business:

> While some business leaders may have a first-instinct shrug when it comes to employee engagement, it offers scores of benefits for companies. In a 2012 report that compiled 263 research studies across 192 companies, Gallup found that companies in the top quartile for engaged employees, compared with the bottom quartile, had 22 percent higher profitability, 10 percent higher customer ratings, 28 percent less theft and 48 percent fewer safety incidents. . . . **Desso** CEO Alexander Collog d'Escury called employees a company's "most important resource," while [author and

corporate advisor Andy] Savitz identified employee engagement as "the human thread between sustainability, the triple bottom line and business results."

This study goes on to explore the link between employee engagement and the new paradigm of the triple bottom line of business, incorporating ethical and environmental, alongside financial, goals and metrics for performance. This engagement fosters awareness that can have powerful impact on the organization's stakeholders. The "business cases" for sustainable strategies have in recent years focused on creating cost savings—reducing waste, increasing efficiency, and other approaches are fairly well accepted. But other benefits to the bottom line are just as compelling:

> Employee attraction, engagement and retention has caught up to—if not surpassed—cost savings as the driving factor influencing companies to embrace sustainability goals. . . . The ability to attract and retain really good people partly depends now on how you're managing [the world's] mega challenges. . . . Companies are hearing this in recruiting, even from the millennials who are desperate for jobs.[292]

A 2014 survey of 1,000 workers revealed that 72 percent want to work for a company whose CEO is actively involved in CSR and/or environmental issues, and 93 percent indicated that they would consider leaving their current jobs if offered a position at a company that had an "excellent" corporate reputation. Competition for top talent involves recognizing social and environmental leadership and CSR strategies are competitive advantages.[293]

PricewaterhouseCoopers, the number one on-campus recruiter in the United States, emphasizes this approach: "If you're trying to hire the best and the brightest all over the country, [one of] the distinguishing factors that set us apart from our competitors is that we not only do the sustainability work with our clients, but we do a great deal of it for ourselves."[294] PwC has committed $150 million over five years to drive volunteerism within the company, as part of its strategy to bolster employee engagement around sustainability and social impact. The program involves PwC providing financial literacy lesson plans for students of all ages. The approach is integrated in important ways, with one executive noting, "What we've seen is the leaders of our 20-something offices compete on how many hours they can get volunteered to deliver the . . . program, so it's actually a core success metric for our most senior partners."[295] The program is seen as critical to the long-term success of the firm and is an example of the alignment of shared values.

Other corporate examples of promoting volunteerism toward engagement include **Timberland,** which has surpassed 1 million employee volunteer hours served, and **Patagonia,** which provides more than seven different ways for employees to get involved in social and environmental good.[296] Profiles of these approaches note that to achieve success, companies should align these activities with their own core values, and with those of their employees: "If a company isn't allowing its talent to engage in sustainability at the workplace, 'someone else will.'"[297]

> Technology and ubiquitous communication provide all of us with an up-close and personal view of the world's problems. A sense of urgency is accompanied by a realization that our top companies have many tools at their disposal—technologies, networks, the power to convene, resources, and flexibility—to make a tremendous impact. Young people are self-organizing around causes that matter to them, and they are reacting to economic conditions that led to layoffs and slow hiring—it is no wonder tech startups and social ventures are so attractive. Despite the economy's recovery, entrepreneurial pursuits are drawing much of our top talent. Millennials will work for organizations that are impacting the world.

Companies engage in diverse efforts to recruit and manage young talent. Starbucks recently announced that they will provide free online education to thousands of their workers through an arrangement with Arizona State University. Any of the company's 135,000 U.S. employees can participate, even those part-time workers who work 20 hours per week, and are not required to remain with the company. Thus, Starbucks "is, in effect, inviting its workers, from the day they join the company, to study whatever they like, and then leave whenever they like, knowing that many of them, degrees in hand, will leave for better-paying jobs. Even if they did, their experience 'would be a credit to our brand, our reputation and our business,' said chairman and CEO Howard Schultz."[298] Schultz describes his approach as strategic: "I believe it will lower attrition, it'll increase performance, it'll attract and retain better people."[299] For years, Starbucks has consistently incorporated innovative strategies such as providing health care to even part-time workers, and giving stock options to employees: "Whether in spite of these perks or because of them, the company has been highly successful; its stock . . . has grown more than a hundredfold since it went public in 1992."[300]

Deloitte presents results of an annual survey of thousands of millennials to learn and share best practices in managing and developing young talent toward company goals. By engaging the voices of this young cohort, they contribute to developing effective strategies for engagement in a meaningful way. Their findings drive their internal approaches, and influence those of their clients.

A final tip: Companies can consider a wealth of information on integrating social and environmental impact considerations provided by Net Impact (*www.netimpact.org*) including suggestions from a recent report on a national study of student and young professional preferences and corporate activities.[301] *Students and new professionals* are encouraged to explicitly consider their values as they seek alignment with their professional choices, enhancing communication abilities and "voice" to maximize engagement with colleagues and supervisors around values, and "walking the talk" of connecting values with the decisions and actions undertaken in the job search and in our work, applying our skills to work with impact—an approach that clearly enhances satisfaction and productivity at work. *Employers* are encouraged to clearly define and articulate the organization's mission, and then "connect the dots" between mission and the work of every employee in every department. Employees must understand how their skills can connect to mission and impact. Further, recruiting for mission will offer a competitive advantage to attracting and retaining the best talent. Connecting jobs to purpose benefits the employee and their managers—and the company's stakeholders, broadly defined.

Conclusion

All photographs used with permission,
Copyright © 2014 by Della Dewald

Millennials and their managers have much reason for optimism in today's
workplace. Millennial desires, characteristics, strengths, and interests
can be channeled toward ethical, effective leadership, and can positively
impact business in myriad ways. These young professionals are posed to
contribute greatly to the new paradigm of our ethical companies. The
potential for positive impact of business in society has never been greater,
and our emerging businesspeople are motivated and enthusiastic about
meeting the challenges ahead. Millennials and their managers can use
Giving Voice to Values (GVV) as one helpful framework for ethical, effective professional development. Millennials can acknowledge and develop
their interests toward effective and ethical organizational functioning,
and managers can foster this development toward shared goals and
organizational impact.

We can briefly revisit the GVV pillars and consider how each can serve as prompts for engagement and leadership development. *Values* can be a galvanizing topic for engagement and commitment at work, and when we acknowledge *choice,* and *normalize* ethical considerations in the workplace, we are setting the stage for successful ethical decision making and action. When we explicitly incorporate notions of *purpose,* starting with consideration of *self-knowledge and alignment* with organizational values, and recognizing and considering strategies to confront the *reasons and rationalizations* for ethically questionable behavior together with colleagues and with our professional role models, we cultivate effective voicing of our values and our greater purpose for professional life.

What will the future of business look like, with these millennials in full force, and in leadership? Forbes magazine recently asked, *What sort of changes will this new generation bring to the workplace?* "Like it or not, the millennials will soon be running the place. The oldest millennials are entering their mid-thirties and are starting to assert new leadership of corporate America,"[302] and reflect this reimagining of business with characteristics including leveling of hierarchies, consistent attention to corporate social responsibility, and more transparent and engaged workplaces.

So as more and more students study business, we can ask, as others have done: "Does the world need more MBAs?" The answer is a resounding yes:

> We need world leaders who deeply understand markets, their connection to the public sector, and the philosophical, cultural and social implications of business's growing global influence. . . . We need leaders who are ready to confront the challenges of growing income inequality, unemployment, environmental impact, and cultural homogenization that current business practices do not yet adequately address . . . who can leverage the power of markets to create lasting social value.[303]

Our young people have the capacities to be these new leaders. Employers and their young employees must meet in the middle. We can and should embrace the millennial tendency to "shine a light" on values and culture at work. In this era in which transparency and high stakes demand innovative solutions, corporations will do well to engage millennials for ethical leadership. My best wishes along the way!

"A Tale of Two Stories" Facilitator Debrief Questions/Reflection

Please note this information is an optional supplement to the "Tale of Two Stories" Exercise, provided as the "Action Item" in Chapter 1. A handout for the small groups is included at the end of this exercise. If facilitators choose, they may reproduce this handout and distribute it to participants at the start of the small group discussions.

Instructions for Small Groups[304]

Prior to these discussions, the group should commit to ground rules of confidentiality; nevertheless, individuals should disguise or omit names of organizations and, certainly, of individuals.

- Go around the circle and tell the story of when you *did* act on your values, taking about 5 minutes each. After everyone has had the chance to tell their stories briefly, the group can share and discuss their answers to the follow-up questions about impact, motivation, satisfaction, and possible enablers, both within and outside of their control.
  - What are some of the similarities, differences, and potential generalizations you see?

This material has been included with permission from the *Giving Voice to Values* curriculum collection www.GivingVoiceToValues.org and www.MaryGentile.com, developed by Mary C. Gentile. The Aspen Institute was founding partner, along with the Yale School of Management, and incubator for *Giving Voice to Values* (GVV). Now funded by Babson College.

- Then consider the second story—the time when you did *not* voice your values. You do not need to actually share this story but, rather, focus your comments upon why the outcome was different. Why didn't you voice and act upon your values? What was different about motivation, satisfaction, and possible enablers?
  - Knowing what enabled you (and your group members) to voice your values in the first stories, what might you be able to do to change the outcome in this second story if faced with such a situation again?

In Large Group

- First of all, do you have any general observations about this exercise? Were some things harder or easier to talk about? Why? Any surprises?
- What appeared to be the strongest **motivators** to speak/act? (Avoiding fears? Pursuing hopes?)
- Did you see any generalizations about when and why folks felt that it was **possible** to speak/act on their values?
- Did you see any generalizations about when and why folks felt that it was **not possible** to speak/act on their values?
- When were folks most satisfied with their choices? Why?
  - When consistent with values?
  - When "successful"? (How do you define "success" in this response?)
  - When acting with or against your "type"? (When acting consistently with their self-image and/or playing to their strengths?)
  - Both?
- Is there anything different about voicing and acting on your viewpoint and values when the issue has an ethical character to it, as opposed to other types of disagreements? What are the differences? Why do you think that there are differences? Does this suggest any strategic fixes?
- What would have made it easier to speak/act?

- Things within your own control:
  - Allies
  - Selection and sequencing of audiences
  - Greater confidence in viewpoint due to securing more information
  - Starting with questions rather than assertions
  - Greater understanding of others' motivations/needs/fears
  - One-on-one or group discussions (i.e., offline conversations with dissenters or key supporters)
  - Working through incremental steps
  - Changing the frame: opportunity versus risk, for example, or as "learning dialogue"
  - Finding win/win solutions
  - Questioning assumptions/professional rationalizations/"truisms" ("The Market made me do it;" "I'll behave differently when I'm in charge;" "The Invisible Hand takes all costs into account so I don't have to;" "Business is a meritocracy so therefore its painful impacts are justified;" and so on)
  - Appealing to shared purpose and/or values (i.e., appeal to alignment)
  - Normalizing (Managing this kind of conflict is part of doing the job. I should learn to do so effectively.)
  - Playing to one's own strengths
- Things within the control of others? (i.e., boss, coworkers, reports, outside parties, organizational systems, or culture)
  - Explicit policies/values
  - Value placed on open debate/discussion
  - Mechanisms for open debate/discussion
  - Systems for raising questions
  - Consistent and visible track record

Optional Follow-up Exercise

Now turn back to your small groups and invite a willing participant to share a story for which the group will craft an effective script and strategy for voicing and acting on his or her values. (Facilitators can use some of the short cases included in this volume as contingency cases, in the event that no one wants to share their own story.)

The small groups can consider the following questions as they work on a response to the story selected:

Clarity of Purpose

- What is your personal purpose in this situation? What is important to you? What are your guiding values?
- What is the organization's purpose in this situation? What is important to it? What are its guiding values?
- What is the purpose of the individual(s) who asked you to take the action that conflicted with your values?
- Are these purposes clear? Do they conflict? Can you find an alignment among them?

Data and Process

- What kind of data do you need to gather in order to plan and act responsibly and effectively?
- What are your action choices in this situation? Which would be most effective? What do you need to be successful? (Consider the organization's culture and programs, as well as your own skills, style, and relationships.)

Scripts

- What are the main arguments you are trying to counter?
- What is at stake for each key player?
- What levers can you use to influence those who disagree with you?

- What is the most powerful and persuasive response to the arguments you want to counter? To whom should the argument be made? When and in what context?
- Back in the large group, each small team shares its challenge and response and the large group engages in collective peer coaching to fine-tune/improve the approach.[305]

Conclusion

- The lessons from this exercise are individual and organizational; strategic and tactical; cognitive and emotional.
- They allow us to define
  - our **individual** motivators and inhibitors;
  - the **organizational** motivators and inhibitors that we want to find and/or develop; the **skills** we want to develop and the **individual strengths** to which we want to play.

Handout for Small Groups

In Groups of Five

Select a **Time Keeper** and **Note Taker** and **Reporter.**

Reporters should be prepared to summarize the generalizations about: what factors enabled folks to voice/act on their values ("enablers"); what prevented them from doing so ("disablers"); and what ideas the group generated for responding to and transforming the "disablers."

(1) Go around the circle and share a story of when you did act on your values. (5 participants with 5 minutes each) *25 minutes*

(2) After everyone has had the chance to tell their story briefly, spend about 10 minutes sharing your answers to the first set of questions. **What are some of the generalizations you see?** *10 minutes*

(3) Then consider your second story—the time you did *not* voice your values. You do not need to tell this story but rather focus your comments upon why the outcome was different. **What was different?**

Knowing what enabled you (and your group members) to voice your values in the first stories, **what might you do to change the outcome in the second story, if faced with such a situation again?** *10 minutes*

Prior to these discussions, the group should establish ground rules of *confidentiality*; nevertheless, individuals should disguise or omit names of organizations and, certainly, of individuals.

APPENDIX B

Personal–Professional Profile

Mary C. Gentile, PhD, Director
www.GivingVoicetoValues.org

Giving *Voice* to Values

Self-Knowledge and Self-Image

As discussed in the note, "Ways of Thinking about Our Values in the Workplace,"[1] one of the most powerful enablers to voicing and acting on our values is an acute self-awareness – such that we know and can play to our strengths, and similarly know and can pre-arrange antidotes to our limitations. Another powerful enabler is a compelling "self-story" that allows us to be clear about who we are and want to be, in advance of encountering value conflicts. In this way, we can anticipate the situations that will be most challenging to us, as individuals, and pre-script ourselves so that we will be less susceptible to the pressures around us.

In order to develop this self-awareness and compelling "self-story" that supports our efforts to voice our values, a number of self-assessment exercises are included here. , There are many other self-assessment tools that one can use for this purpose, in addition to those listed below. The point is to know ourselves and to preemptively script the self-story that will best support our efforts to voice our values.

Sample Exercises

- **"Personal-Professional Profile"**
This self-assessment profile draws on questions from the Aspen Institute Business and Society Program (Aspen BSP) *MBA Student Attitudes Survey* which invites respondents to consider the role of business and business leaders in society, and some common and/or current values conflicts that managers may face with regard to fulfilling that role. The list of values conflicts in question 3 can be revised and updated to reflect current conditions as appropriate. Responses to questions 1 and 3 through 7 can be compared to the MBA student responses Aspen BSP obtained when they ran this survey.

The Personal-Professional Profile also includes a number of questions that invite respondents to consider their own personal sense of purpose and their image of themselves at their best.

Finally, this Profile invites students to consider their own predispositions around risk, communication style, loyalty, and self-image, as discussed in "Ways of Thinking about Our Values in the Workplace."

---

[1] See www.GivingVoiceToValues.org

This material has been included with permission from the *Giving Voice to Values* curriculum collection www.GivingVoiceToValues.org and www.MaryGentile.com, developed by Mary C. Gentile. The Aspen Institute was founding partner, along with the Yale School of Management, and incubator for *Giving Voice to Values* (GVV). Now funded by Babson College.

- **"Reflected Best Self Exercise"**

An excellent self-assessment tool that may be adapted for use in the ***Giving Voice to Values*** curriculum is the "Reflected Best Self Exercise," from the Center for Positive Organizational Scholarship at the University Of Michigan Ross School Of Business (by Robert E. Quinn, Jane E. Dutton and Gretchen M. Spreitzer, Product # 001B). The abstract of this exercise states:

"The Reflected Best Self exercise provides feedback to participants about who they are when they are at their best. Participants request positive feedback from significant people in their lives, which they then synthesize into a cumulative portrait of their "best self." The exercise can be used as a tool for personal development because it provides valuable insights into the ways a person adds value and makes a contribution."

Although the exercise is designed to capture the participant's "best self" stories in general, the survey protocol could be adapted to ask for specific stories when the individual had most effectively or courageously voiced his or her values in a challenging situation.

- **"Framing A Life Story"** (*Giving Voice to Values*)

A brief reading and discussion guide that invites participants to craft the "life story" that will help support them in their practice of voicing their values.

- **Decision Making Bias Survey**

As preparation for the discussions in "Scripts and Skills," participants may wish to complete the "Reader Survey" at the start of *The Psychology of Judgment and Decision Making* by Scott Plous (McGraw-Hill, Inc., 1993).

Personal-Professional Profile[2]

1. In your definition of a "well-run" company, how important are the following?
Please indicate whether each one of the following is "very important," "somewhat important," or "not important at all."

a.) Provides excellent customer service
Very important   Somewhat important   Not important at all

b.) Has efficient and flexible operations
Very important   Somewhat important   Not important at all

c.) Offers high financial return to shareholders
Very important   Somewhat important   Not important at all

d.) Attracts and retains exceptional people
Very important   Somewhat important   Not important at all

e.) Creates products or services that benefit society
Very important   Somewhat important   Not important at all

f.) Adheres to a strong mission
Very important   Somewhat important   Not important at all

g.) Invests in employee training and professional development
Very important   Somewhat important   Not important at all

h.) Operates according to its values and a strong code of ethics
Very important   Somewhat important   Not important at all

i.) Is a stable employer
Very important   Somewhat important   Not important at all

j.) Provides competitive compensation
Very important   Somewhat important   Not important at all

k.) Adheres to progressive environmental policies
Very important   Somewhat important   Not important at all

l.) Produces high-quality products and services
Very important   Somewhat important   Not important at all

---

[2] The first 14 questions in this profile were piloted at the University of Texas-Austin in 2003. Questions 1 and 3-7 are taken and/or adapted from The Aspen Institute Business and Society Program Student Attitudes Survey (www.aspenbsp.org). Questions 10-14 are adapted from *The Power of Full Engagement* by Jim Loehr and Tony Schwartz (The Free Press, 2003). Questions 15-19 are based on the *Giving Voice to Values* interview findings.

2. Would you add something to the above list that you think is "very important"? If so, what?

3. Which of the following issues pose the greatest challenges for today's CEOs and senior executives?

Please choose a maximum of three alternatives.
____ Lack of investor confidence
____ Increased activism on the part of environmental and social advocacy groups
____ Corporate scandal (e.g., accounting misstatements, conflict of interest)
____ Questions about executive compensation levels and incentive systems
____ Breakdown in trust between employees and management
____ Inadequate regulatory and legal institutions
____ Product safety and liability
____ Economic downturn
____ Growing inequity in the distribution of wealth around the world
____ Lack of public trust in business
____ Managing international supply chain requirements
____ War and international instability
____ Threat of terrorism
____ Other (please specify)

4. To what extent do you agree or disagree with the following statements?
Please indicate whether you "strongly agree," "somewhat agree," "somewhat disagree," or "strongly disagree" with each of the following statements:

a.) Business people are more likely to care about the social responsibilities of companies when the economy is strong.
Strongly agree   Somewhat agree   Somewhat disagree   Strongly disagree

b.) When a multi-national company is entering a new market in a less-developed country, it has a responsibility to go above and beyond business success and contribute to the development of the local community.
Strongly agree   Somewhat agree   Somewhat disagree   Strongly disagree

c.) When it comes to the environment, all a company has to do is to comply with the law.
Strongly agree   Somewhat agree   Somewhat disagree   Strongly disagree

d.) Companies should maintain their employees' job security even if they incur a short-term drop in profit as a result.
Strongly agree   Somewhat agree   Somewhat disagree   Strongly disagree

e.) Most companies accurately report their earnings and profits.
Strongly agree   Somewhat agree   Somewhat disagree   Strongly disagree

f.) Corporate reputation is important to me in making my decision about the organization where I want to work.
Strongly agree   Somewhat agree   Somewhat disagree   Strongly disagree

g.) Managers place too much emphasis on short-term performance measures when making business decisions.
Strongly agree   Somewhat agree   Somewhat disagree   Strongly disagree

h.) I anticipate that my own values will sometimes conflict with what I am asked to do in business.
Strongly agree   Somewhat agree   Somewhat disagree   Strongly disagree

5. **If you answered the above statement "4h" with "somewhat agree" or "strongly agree," please specify which kinds of values conflicts you expect to face:**

6. **Assume you are engaged in each of the following business activities/practices. How likely do you think it is that values conflicts would arise?**
Please indicate whether it is "very likely," "somewhat likely," or "not likely at all" that values conflicts would arise.

a.) Managing personnel in manufacturing facilities/ plants
Very likely   Somewhat likely   Not likely at all

b.) Outsourcing production operations
Very likely   Somewhat likely   Not likely at all

c.) Investing in less-developed countries
Very likely   Somewhat likely   Not likely at all

d.) Downsizing
Very likely   Somewhat likely   Not likely at all

e.) Financial reporting
Very likely   Somewhat likely   Not likely at all

f.) Natural resource exploration
Very likely   Somewhat likely   Not likely at all

g.) Awarding stock options
Very likely   Somewhat likely   Not likely at all

h.) Setting executive compensation levels
Very likely   Somewhat likely   Not likely at all

i.) Conducting performance reviews
Very likely   Somewhat likely   Not likely at all

j.) Interacting with government officials
Very likely   Somewhat likely   Not likely at all

k.) Raising or borrowing capital
Very likely   Somewhat likely   Not likely at all

l.) Negotiating with suppliers or customers
Very likely   Somewhat likely   Not likely at all

7. **If you find that your values conflict with those of the company where you work, how likely is it that you will:**
Please indicate whether it is "very likely," "somewhat likely," or "not likely at all"

a.) Not mind too much
Very likely   Somewhat likely   Not likely at all

b.) Experience it as stressful
Very likely   Somewhat likely   Not likely at all

c.) Quietly handle the stress
Very likely   Somewhat likely   Not likely at all

d.) Look for another job
Very likely   Somewhat likely   Not likely at all

e.) Speak up about your objections
Very likely   Somewhat likely   Not likely at all

f.) Advocate alternative values or approaches within the company
Very likely   Somewhat likely   Not likely at all

g.) Try to get others to join you in addressing your concerns
Very likely   Somewhat likely   Not likely at all

8. Think of a few occasions when you encountered a values conflict in your previous work experience. Recall how you handled the situations. Would you characterize yourself and your behavior as that of:[3]

____**an Idealist** (One who is primarily concerned with moral ideals when making decisions on how to act.)

____**a Pragmatist** (One who is concerned with his/her own material welfare, but also with moral ideals. "Pragmatists will gladly do their fair share to create a civil society, but not place themselves at a systematic disadvantage" to do so.)

____**an Opportunist** (One who is only concerned with his/her own material welfare.)

9. If you placed yourself in the category of "pragmatist," what can you do to maximize the likelihood that you will act on your ideals? What competencies will you need?

10. Think of someone you deeply respect. What are the 2 or 3 characteristics you most admire in this person?

11. Who are you at your best?

12. Name your 3 or 4 deepest values.

---

[3] Categories and descriptions drawn from Gregory Dees and Peter Crampton, "Shrewd Bargaining on the Moral Frontier: Toward a Theory of Morality in Practice", *Business Ethics Quarterly*, April 1991, vol. 1, no. 2, p. 146 and 164.

13. **What is the one sentence you would like to see in your obituary that captures who you really were in your life?**

14. Questions of Purpose:
What is your personal purpose for your business career?

- Some possible issues to consider:
- What impact do you want to have? On whom?
- Whom do you want to know you benefited? In what ways?
- What do you want to learn?
- How do you define your impact as a/n: auditor, investor, manager, product developer, marketer, senior executive, etc.?
- What do you hope to accomplish? What will make your professional life worthwhile?
- How do you want to feel about yourself and your work, both while you are doing it and in the end?

15. Questions of Risk

a.) Are you a risk-taker or risk-averse?

b.) What are the greatest risks you face in your line of work? Are they personal (e.g., livelihood, deportation, legal punishment) or are they professional (e.g., harm to customers, employees, the firm), or are they societal (e.g., impact on environment, profession, industry, nation)?

c.) What levels of risk can and can't you live with?

16. Questions of Personal Communication Style/Preference:

a.) Do you deal well with conflict or are you non-confrontational? Under what circumstances do you behave in each way?

b.) Do you prefer communicating in person or in writing?

c.) Do you think best from the gut and in-the-moment or do you need to take time out to reflect and craft your communications?

d.) Do you assert your position with statements or do you use questions to communicate?

17. Questions of Loyalty:

a.) Do you tend to feel the greatest loyalty to family; work colleagues; your firm/employer; or to other stakeholders, such as customers?

b.) Under what conditions and given what stakes?

18. Questions of Self-Image:

a.) Do you see yourself as shrewd or naïve?

b.) As idealistic or pragmatic?

c.) As a learner or as a teacher?

d.) Other?

PERSONAL-PROFESSIONAL PROFILE: FACULTY DEBRIEF

- Distribute the "Personal Professional Profile" and invite students to complete it. Assure them that they will not be asked to turn it in but will be invited to share some of their thoughts verbally.[10 MINS]
- After they have completed the profile, invite students to break into groups of 5 or 6 and discuss the following questions: [20 MINS]
  - Which of these questions were most difficult for you to answer? Why?
  - Taking a look at questions 5 and 6, what generalizations can you draw about where you expect values conflicts to be most challenging?
  - Taking a look at questions 7 and 9, which skills do you think will be necessary to deal with values challenges in the workplace?
  - If you are willing, share your personal purpose statements and see whether there are any generalizations you can draw from comparing them.

Faculty can bring students back to large group and invite them to share their answers to the above questions. Then faculty can share the Aspen BSP data from the same survey, handing out the Executive Summaries[4] and inviting students to review it at their leisure and see where they agree or disagree.

- Faculty can ask: Keeping your own personal statement of purpose for your business career in mind, you might want to consider Charles Handy's response to the question, "What's a Business For?" about the wider purpose of business:

  "Both sides of the Atlantic would agree that there is, first, a clear and important need to meet the expectations of a company's theoretical owners: the shareholders. It would, however, be more accurate to call most of them investors, perhaps even gamblers. They have none of the pride or responsibility of ownership and are, if truth be told, only there for the money. Nevertheless, if management fails to meet their financial hopes, the share price will fall, exposing the company to unwanted predators and making it more difficult to raise new finance *But to turn shareholders' needs into a purpose is to be guilty of a logical confusion, to mistake a necessary condition for a sufficient one.* We need to eat to live; food is a necessary condition of life. But if we lived mainly to eat, making food a sufficient or sole purpose of life, we would become gross. *The purpose of business is not to make a profit, full stop. It is to make a profit so that the business can do something more or better.*" **Charles Handy** (emphasis added)[5]

- What do you think of Handy's response? If you accepted it, how might it affect your decision making? What might be some examples of the "something more or better" that he mentions? (Students should be encouraged to respond honestly, whether they agree or disagree. The point is to simply suggest an alternative way of thinking about the usual answer to this question.)

- As we discuss the purpose of business, it is important to keep in mind the current business context as well:

---

[4] This survey and the response data can be obtained from The Aspen Institute Business & Society Program, www.aspenbsp.org.

[5] "What's a Business For?" by Charles Handy. *Harvard Business Review* (December 2002, Reprint #R0212C), p. 5.

"A Gallup poll conducted early this year [2002] found that 90% of Americans felt that people running corporations could not be trusted to look after the interest of their employees, and only 18% thought that corporations looked after their shareholders a great deal. Forty-three percent, in fact, believed that senior executives were only in it for themselves. In Britain, that figure, according to another poll, was 95%."
Charles Handy

- Does this type of business environment make it easier or more difficult to find a public market for ethical and responsible management behavior?
  - In other words, does this kind of context mean that employees, consumers, communities, voters, etc. are too skeptical to give managers the benefit of the doubt?
  - Or, does it mean that they will be eager to reward those managers who prove them wrong?
  - What competencies does a manager need to thrive in such a world?

- Your answers to questions 14-19 should provide background for considering the "Framing a Life Story" exercise, as well as a roadmap for considering your strengths and challenges in building the capacity to voice and act on your values in the workplace. Hang onto this profile and re-visit it as you develop "scripts" for responding to value conflicts.
  - For example, to pursue discussions of Communications Style and Self-Image, instructors may use other *Giving Voice to Values* materials such as The Diversity Consultant (A) and (B)" and "Lisa Baxter: Developing a Voice
  - To pursue discussions of Risk, instructors may use "The Price (A) and (B)."
  - To pursue discussion of Purpose, instructors may use "A Personal Struggle with the Definition of Success."

- As you consider the different definitions of business purpose that can be observed today, as well as your own personal statement of career purpose, it's probably become apparent that you are likely to face situations in your career where it won't be easy to align these two. *Giving Voice to Values* is about developing the kinds of competencies necessary to do just that. These competencies include the ability to really listen to the positions and values of others as well as to speak clearly and persuasively on behalf of your own. It is helpful to hear from folks who have faced this kind of challenge in their careers and to take the opportunity to reconsider the times when you have done so yourself.

APPENDIX C

A Framework for Ethical Decision Making

We've described the *Giving Voice to Values* (GVV) approach as post-decision making—after one decides what to do in the face of a values conflict, how does one go about getting it done in a given context? While this action orientation is the focus of this volume, the following model is provided for reference. Most ethics courses and trainings include discussion of a decision model for determining ethical action. These models are designed to operationalize the philosophical principles of ethical decision making, to encourage exploration of stakeholders and impact, and ultimately to equip the actor to make a principled, reasoned decision. The steps are quite clear—but consider how often they are ignored! Exploring and discussing such a model can be an invigorating and useful exercise for professional development. The progression to the GVV considerations then follows.

I have adapted this model from the works of Robert Audi[306] and Joseph DesJardins[307], among others, and included elements that facilitate ready transition to the next step—applying the action orientation of the GVV approach. I use this model with my students, and add a critical step that is often missing in examples of these decision models: that of communicating your decision to stakeholders. As my students and I discuss, the ability to articulate and explain your reasoning is fundamental to business leadership.

The intention is not to imply the need for a pen-and-paper, systematic analysis of decision making, minor and major, at every turn. Rather, as we have said with GVV, the intention is to develop our muscle around principled decision making. The more we are explicit and intentional about this process, the more it becomes part of who we are, every day.

(1) Who has a stake in this decision? What is at stake for each of them?

(2) Which ethical obligations are relevant? (here we might consider Audi's discussion of moral obligations[a]—aligned with our earlier discussion of universal values)

(3) How might these obligations conflict with one another?

(4) What guidance is available? Are there resources (codes of conduct, legal requirements, trusted allies, institutional or personal support) that we can consider when formulating our decision?

(5) What are our options? What are the alternative resolutions we can identify for this decision?

(6) How would we articulate this decision to stakeholders?

(7) A final check—can this decision be considered universalizable? Can it be used as a guiding precedent for future decisions?

(8) What should be done?

---

[a]Audi provides the following list, adapted in part from the work of W.D. Ross, as a summary of our moral obligations: *justice, non-injury, fidelity, veracity, reparation, beneficence, self-improvement, gratitude, liberty, respectfulness.*

APPENDIX D

Case Studies

Case studies, based on real experiences, are powerful tools for professional development, particularly when explored with peers and colleagues. Brief leadership development workshops can be offered that present these case studies for interactive discussion, or they can be integrated into existing trainings or other opportunities for professional learning.

Giving Voice to Values (GVV) cases are unique in that they presuppose the resolution—the question for learners is not, as in traditional case studies, *what should be done?* These explorations of how to resolve ethical issues can be effectively enhanced by use of decision-making models, for example, the one provided in Appendix C. In GVV cases, however, the question is one of action. Thus, after the protagonist has determined what he/she wants to do, *how, in a given context, can he/she effectively get it done?* These action-oriented cases are well aligned for use with millennials. Readers are encouraged to consider exploring these and other discussion prompts. Managers or other discussion facilitators might consider presenting these cases for team discussion as part of existing training opportunities, or dedicating a session to exploring these or similar dilemmas at work. Case studies, role plays, and other activities can reinforce corporate goals and values in an engaging way.

Cases included here were originally published in the GVV collection. Many more are available, on topics by industry, professional role, and job function. See www.GivingVoiceToValues.org for more information.

Part A of these cases, all based on actual experiences and several co-authored with my millennial students, describes a specific dilemma in business and sets the stage for discussion. *Part B* cases, which describe what actually happened as the case was resolved, along with *Discussion Guidelines* including Q&A and "teaching notes" that may help facilitate the discussion, are available through the GVV collection—open source with no fee for use, with permission.

We hope that these can be tools to facilitate discussion, ideally in multigenerational group settings at work. Participants can exchange ideas and explore options for effective, ethical action. The following questions can help guide efforts to explore cases, either those generated from within individual companies, or those provided by the GVV curriculum. Guidelines are adapted from the GVV curriculum.

Discussion Guidelines

Three Lenses

- As decision maker in the case, what is our level and role within the organization?
  - Available actions differ depending on our role and level—strategies and tactics differ depending on level of responsibility and degree of influence/authority.
- What motivates us? What motivates or drives the other relevant actors in the situation? In other words, what is at stake for each of us?
  - It is important and useful to pursue self-knowledge in advance of challenging situations when our judgment might be clouded.
  - It is important and useful to anticipate and develop external (and internal) mechanisms to correct for anticipated self-bias.
  - It is important and useful to test our assumptions about the perspectives and motivations of others.
- What are the commonly heard "reasons and rationalizations" for being less than honest in reporting, and what are some possible responses (levers) to them?

OR

- What are the main arguments you are trying to counter? That is, what are the reasons and rationalizations you need to address?

- What is at stake for the key parties, including those who disagree with you?
- What levers can you use to influence those who disagree with you?
- What is your most powerful and persuasive response to the reasons and rationalizations you need to address? To whom should the argument be made? When and in what context?

Cases

"A Billing Bind"

A summer intern at a small public accounting firm confronts overbilling client hours.

"Is This My Place"

A new manager questions the appropriateness of valuation policies.

"Trusting the Trust Accounts"

A summer intern in the trust department of a local community bank questions the bank's investment strategies with respect to customer's trust accounts.

"Inflating Value"

A summer intern at a prestigious New York investment bank is asked to prepare potentially inaccurate valuation information for a major deal.

Mary C. Gentile, PhD, Director
www.GivingVoicetoValues.org

Giving *Voice* to Values

A Billing Bind (A)[1]

When she received an offer for a summer internship from a small, local public accounting firm, Gabby felt both excited and relieved. She hoped this would be a backup plan in the event her other more preferred option did not work out. When this in fact became the case, she knew the summer would not be exactly as she had hoped; however, she was prepared to use it as a learning experience to become better acquainted with the accounting profession. The firm was small and no other interns were hired for that specific branch that summer. Because the branch also had few young employees, Gabby did not really feel as though she had peers at the office. The summer passed slowly and uneventfully, with one exception.

Occasionally, a few of the more senior accountants who had extra work would allow Gabby to help them with some of the less significant tasks. Generally these jobs were not for specific clients and were more administrative in nature. However, once in a while, the assignments required Gabby to bill the clients for the tasks she performed based on the time she spent doing the work. At the time she started the internship, she was assigned a buddy – Todd – who explained basic firm policies to her and showed her how to use the company's client account and billing system. Todd also showed Gabby how to record the time she spent working and how to bill it to certain clients.

About halfway through the summer, Todd sent out an email to the entire group detailing a project which he was managing. The accounting firm was moving from paper-based files to an electronic database and the recent paper files needed to be scanned into the computers. The firm's employees recognized this as secondary and uninteresting work, which they readily delegated to Gabby. The work was simple and quick and each client's paperwork usually took

---

[1] Developed by Ellen Mrowka and Jessica McManus Warnell, University of Notre Dame, with Karen Whelan-Berry, Providence College. This case was inspired by an actual internship experience but names and other situational details have been changed, and interview sources left uncredited with permission, for confidentiality and teaching purposes.

This material has been included with permission from the *Giving Voice to Values* curriculum collection www.GivingVoiceToValues.org and www.MaryGentile.com, developed by Mary C. Gentile and from E. Mrowka and J. McManus Warnell. The Aspen Institute was founding partner, along with the Yale School of Management, and incubator for *Giving Voice to Values* (GVV). Now funded by Babson College.

less than 15 minutes. However, in Todd's original email to the group, he required each client to be billed for a half hour's worth of work.

Gabby quickly realized that the clients were being billed for more work than was actually being performed. Further, she knew that her billable rate was much lower than that of the senior accountants initially expected to do the work as understood by the clients. Without any true peers, there really was no one for her to consult on this matter to determine if this blanket policy was acceptable as common practice. Gabby's initial reaction was that overcharging clients, especially those smaller ones, could not be ethically correct. She was not sure who to turn to, if anyone. Since this summer job was not something she wanted to transition into a future career, Gabby questioned if raising this concern was worth the while.

Gabby knew what she should do and wanted to act on her instincts. But how could Gabby question authority effectively and safely? With whom should she speak, and what should she say?

Mary C. Gentile, PhD, Director
www.GivingVoicetoValues.org

Giving _Voice_ to Values

Is This My Place? ...Speaking "UP" (A)[1]

Ben was pleased when he was hired out of college, with an accounting degree, to manage the internal and external reporting for a non-profit organization whose work he respected. The organization collected donations of medical supplies from U.S. producers and shipped them to developing countries where the need was great and where they had partnerships with service providers on the ground.

It was a small, thinly-staffed office and that also appealed to Ben. He knew their small size was the reason he had the opportunity to take on so much responsibility so quickly, and he approved of the thin operating expenses. The more efficient their operations, the greater the services they could provide to the individuals who most needed them.

However, shortly after starting work, he began to see the downside of the organization's thin staffing. The Executive Director was over-worked and stressed. Although by nature a micro-manager, necessity dictated that she delegate everything she could to her staff. And he quickly began to recognize that the organization had no formal system for monitoring the value of donated supplies for tax purposes. They relied on donors who might feel pressures from their own organizations to inflate the values.

Ben struggled with several questions at first: shouldn't he just trust the donors? After all, they were engaging in corporate philanthropy. And how much did it really matter? The point was to get the supplies to those who needed them overseas. He didn't want to do anything that would discourage the donations. And he felt confident his Executive Director was aware of the conflict but just didn't see it as a priority. In fact, when instructing staff on what she needed from them with regard to reporting, she often commented that she wasn't interested in "data," but rather focused on relationships and real world impacts. Wouldn't she know better than he did how to prioritize this issue? And where was the organization's accountant on this question?

On the other hand, as time went on, Ben became quite certain that some of their donors were deceiving the IRS, and that he – and his organization – were enabling that deception. He knew he didn't want to be part of that.

---

[1] This case was inspired by interviews and observations of actual experiences but names and other situational details have been changed for confidentiality and teaching purposes.

This material has been included with permission from the _Giving Voice to Values_ curriculum collection www.GivingVoiceToValues.org and www.MaryGentile.com, developed by Mary C. Gentile. The Aspen Institute was founding partner, along with the Yale School of Management, and incubator for _Giving Voice to Values_ (GVV). Now funded by Babson College.

And although he was young, he was a cocky sort. In fact, it had been his outspoken identification of an accounting error during his interview that had secured him the job in the first place, despite his relative youth. Of course, that error was simply a mistake and had had no ethical implications.

What should he say, to whom, when and how?

Mary C. Gentile, PhD, Director
www.GivingVoicetoValues.org

Giving *Voice* to Values

Trusting the Trust Accounts (A)[1]

Billy was excited to start his summer internship in the Trust Department at a local, publicly-traded community bank. He had just completed his junior year majoring in Finance at a highly ranked undergraduate university and he was looking forward to applying the skills he had learned in his classes. His internship started in early June, and Billy spent the first few days getting to know the systems of the bank and the five other employees in the Trust Department. He also helped the staff within the Trust Department with minor tasks. Billy was able to quickly form relationships with the other employees. He wanted to display his interest and enthusiasm, so he made a point of reaching out to each member of the staff with a friendly introduction. In addition, due to the small staff, he was able to quickly form a strong relationship with his immediate supervisor, Joe, who was also a member of the bank's senior management. Joe took Billy out to lunch for his first couple of days at the bank and the two discovered that they both enjoyed golf, which allowed for friendly small talk in the office.

One of Billy's first projects was to monitor the cash sweep balance of the trust accounts. These accounts were comprised of the cash not invested in stocks or bonds, and also included any incoming cash from items such as dividends on investments. For each individual account, the cash sweep account made up a very small percentage of the overall trust account. However, when each of the cash sweep accounts was combined within the Trust Department, the account totaled a much more significant number of nearly $5 million. While the trust sweep balance account made up a relatively small portion of the bank's overall size, the Trust Department was a rapidly growing and profitable division.

---

[1] Developed by John T. Lytle and Jessica McManus Warnell, University of Notre Dame, with Karen Whelan-Berry, Providence College.
This case was inspired by an actual internship experience but names and other situational details have been changed, and interview sources left un-credited with permission, for confidentiality and teaching purposes.

This material has been included with permission from the *Giving Voice to Values* curriculum collection www.GivingVoiceToValues.org and www.MaryGentile.com, developed by Mary C. Gentile and from J. Lytle and J. McManus Warnell. The Aspen Institute was founding partner, along with the Yale School of Management, and incubator for *Giving Voice to Values* (GVV). Now funded by Babson College.

After analyzing the cash balances of the trust accounts for a few days, Billy became curious as to the specific return being generated on the cash sweep balances. He learned that this cash was invested in one of the bank's money market accounts that was earning a very meager rate of return relative to other investment options of the same risk. This finding puzzled Billy because he had learned in many of his classes in the previous semester that maximizing client revenue as well as the bank's revenue was critical to the operations of a successful bank. Billy was concerned that the bank was not maximizing the earning potential of the cash within the trust accounts. He was also worried that the bank may be keeping the cash within the bank by investing the cash balances in a money market account in order to boost the bank's overall size, but at the expense of the client's return. After giving it some thought, Billy thought that the bank may want to keep the money within the bank and increase the bank's apparent assets in order to draw new customers. However, that did not address the fact that the existing customers could be earning a larger return.

Billy felt confident about his opinion about what had been happening with the cash sweep balances of the trust accounts. If his hunch was correct, the bank was not doing all that it could to maximize the earnings of customers. Although he felt sure of his assessment, Billy also felt nervous about sharing his findings because he had only been at the bank for a short time and was an intern. His supervisor, Joe, a member of senior management, had been there for two years, but had nearly twenty years of experience in banking. In addition, the other Trust Officers had each been at the bank for roughly ten years.

Billy knew he should take action. He had recently taken a course in business ethics and he wanted to put into action his skills that he had learned in the class. He also knew that maximizing the investment returns of customers was an important issue, especially given the economic downturn that had negatively affected so many people. But how should Billy raise the issue, and with whom?

Mary C. Gentile, PhD, Director
www.GivingVoicetoValues.org   **Giving *Voice* to Values**

Inflating Value (A)[1]

Jack, a confident and outgoing undergraduate student, had just accepted a summer internship as an analyst at a prestigious investment bank in New York. Jack was an outspoken student in the classroom, never afraid to voice his opinion among his classmates and professors. He was enjoying his internship so far, as this was the career he had wanted to pursue since deciding to focus his undergraduate studies on finance. He had heard stories of the lifestyle of investment banking – completing deals during the day before enjoying the city's finest nightlife in the evening. However, the pace and sense of urgency appeared even more demanding than he had anticipated. And, as he sat at his desk only several weeks into his internship, he realized that in some ways he felt intimidated by the culture of the investment bank.

The office in which Jack was working could be described as the opposite of flat. It was very clear where individuals were on the food chain, if not by the way people spoke to each other, then by office size and/or their wardrobe. There appeared to be an unwritten rule that one could never dress better than anyone at a level above them. Aggressive cutaway collars and French cufflinks were reserved for those above the analyst and, in most cases, the associate level. Jack had noticed this strict hierarchy from the second he walked into the office on his first day.

As he sat in the "bullpen" with countless analysts surrounding him, Jack was called into his Associate's office. As he walked to the meeting with his Associate, he was very aware of the culture and office norms. Jack also knew that in investment banking there is a very strict

---

[1] Developed by Jessica McManus Warnell, University of Notre Dame, with Karen Whelan-Berry, Providence College This case was inspired by an actual internship experience but names and other situational details have been changed, and interview sources left un-credited with permission, for confidentiality and teaching purposes.

This material has been included with permission from the *Giving Voice to Values* curriculum collection www.GivingVoiceToValues.org and www.MaryGentile.com, developed by Mary C. Gentile and from J. McManus Warnell. The Aspen Institute was founding partner, along with the Yale School of Management, and incubator for *Giving Voice to Values* (GVV). Now funded by Babson College.]

hierarchy of command. The managing directors are the most senior bankers who maintain and establish relationships with clients, most of which are huge corporations. Next, are the vice presidents, who typically will lead a particular deal that a managing director passes off to them once he or she secures the business from the client. While a managing director is always on a deal team, the vice president leads its execution within the office. Along with the vice president on a given deal, there is typically an associate and an analyst.

"How's it going, Jack? Why don't you take a seat? I want to loop you in on an exciting deal that I just got staffed on. It's a client of Peter Fisher's and we are also going to be working with Michael Parsons on this one," said David, Jack's Associate. Jack was excited that he had been staffed on a deal team with Fisher, one of the best managing directors in the office, because it was a great opportunity to make a good first impression with him. The associate continued, "So the company we are representing, ABC Lighting, is a manufacturer and marketer of light bulbs of a variety of sizes. Not only do they produce the light bulbs, they also produce the fixtures related to lighting. ABC is looking at opportunities to sell. Given the current economic climate, it has run into some trouble. It originates a lot of its business from new construction and with that market completely bottoming out; its growth projections in the immediate future are not stellar. Additionally, it employs non-LED technology, which is to some extent out of date technology because it is not as energy efficient and just does not produce the same quality of light. What we need you to do, Jack, is to tackle some of the initial analysis. We need you to tell us what this thing is worth, what we can sell it for. Let's focus on comparable multiples analysis taking a look at these companies as its peer group."

David rattled off 15 lighting company names as Jack frantically scribbled the names on a notepad. He was pleased that his research as an intern would be contributing to such a significant decision at the company. "Perfect," Jack responded, "I'll take a look at this right away." As Jack left his associate's office and headed back to his desk, he knew he needed to do a good job on this deal. After all, he had only been there for three weeks and this was his first staffing on a live deal. As he dove into the analysis, Jack was carefully, but quickly gathering the information on ABC's peer group. In this sort of analysis, the analyst will look at the stock trading prices for each comparable company and compare it to some operating metric for that company. For example, if a company is trading at a stock price of $10 per share, and has projected earnings for the next year of $1.00 per share , the company would be trading at a 10 times multiple. As Jack went through the analysis, he realized that the majority of the companies within the peer group which the associate had identified were trading at roughly 13 times earnings per share. Applying this average multiple of 13 times earnings to ABC's projected earnings of $1.50 per share, Jack calculated the appropriate share price for ABC at around $19.50. With 15 million shares outstanding, ABC's equity value and selling price was just under $300 million.

Before Jack reported his findings to his associate, he took a deeper look at some of the companies that were in the peer group to assure that they were truly comparable companies. What Jack found, however, was that none of the companies in the peer group made the light fixtures, only lights. Furthermore, the majority of the comparable companies were actually producers of LED lighting rather than the non-LED lighting which ABC produced. These findings materially changed the valuation Jack had just completed.

Jack went back and repeated the analysis with a peer group he felt was more appropriate, with companies that made both non-LED and LED lighting and a variety of light fixtures. He found that this peer group actually traded at only 6 times earnings per share on average, reflecting the poorer growth opportunities currently present for that segment of the lighting industry. A six times earnings multiple applied to ABC's earnings of $1.50 resulted in a value of $135 million dollars, or $9.00 per share times the 15 million shares outstanding. If Jack didn't say anything, the valuation would be much higher. The greater the valuation, the happier the client and, in turn, the larger the fees the bank would earn. The larger the fee the managing director brings in to the firm, the greater the director's bonus, and as a result, the greater the bonuses for those bankers who helped the director bring in and complete the deals. Should Jack voice his opinion regarding the companies that should make up the peer group for ABC?

Jack sat in the bullpen with his fellow analysts around him frantically cranking out valuations for other deals for other associates, and Jack realized he had a decision to make. The difference between not voicing his opinion and doing so was selling the firm for about $300 million or less than half that much, $135 million. Jack wanted to do the right thing for the investment bank, for ABC, and for his career. As Jack considered his options, he reflected upon how he had spoken out his entire educational life. This thought gave him the confidence to realize that he was doing the right thing if he spoke up about the valuation, but he was still very aware that he was trying to make a good impression to receive a full time offer after graduation. He didn't want to step on any toes but, at the same time, Jack was not comfortable turning over the original peer group and valuation work, which he felt was off by more than $150 million dollars.

What should Jack say and to whom should he voice his opinion? How should he present his discomfort with the original peer group and valuation at around double what he believed the company was truly worth?

Endnotes

1. "The Millennials are Coming," http://www.cbsnews.com/news/the-millennials-are-coming/, accessed November 8, 2007.

2. Gentile, M. C. 2010. *Giving Voice to Values: How to Speak Your Mind When You Know What's Right*. New Haven, CT: Yale University Press.

3. Corporate Survey was conducted online and includes self-reported data which may include minor variations (Spring 2014).

4. http://www.nces.edu/gov, 2014.

5. Kambhampati, S. 2014. "Business is a Big Draw for International Students in the U.S.," *The Chronicle of Higher Education*. http://chronicle.com/blogs/data/2014/08/29/one-in-three-international-undergraduate-students-come-to-the-u-s-to-study-business/.

6. "Schumpeter" Column. 2009. "The Pedagogy of the Privileged," *The Economist 26*. http://www.economist.com/node/14493183.

7. Rest, J. R., Narvaez, D., Bebeau, M., and Thoma, S. J. 1999. *Postconventional Moral Thinking: A Neo-Kohlbergian Approach*. Mahwah, NJ: Lawrence Erlbaum Associates.

    Neubaum, D. O., Pagell, M., Drexler, Jr., J. A., McKee-Ryan, F. M., and Larson, E. 2009. "Business Education and Its Relationship to Student Personal Moral Philosophies and Attitudes Toward Profits: An Empirical Response to Critics," *Journal of Management Learning & Education 8*, no. 1, pp. 9–24.

    Christensen, D., Barnes, J. N., and Rees, D. A. 2007. "Developing Resolve to Have Moral Courage: A Field Comparison of Teaching Methods," *Journal of Business Ethics Education 4*, pp. 79–96.

    Caldwell, C. 2010. "A Ten-Step Model for Academic Integrity: A Positive Approach for Business Schools," *Journal of Business Ethics 92*, pp. 1–13.

8. McManus W. J. 2010. "An Undergraduate Business Ethics Curriculum: Learning and Development Outcomes," *Journal of Business Ethics Education 7*, pp. 63–84.

9. United Nations Global Compact-Accenture CEO Study. 2010. "CEO Reflections on Progress to Date, Challenges Ahead and the Impact of the Journey Toward a Sustainable Economy," http://www.unglobalcompact.org/docs/news_events/8.1/UNGC_Accenture_CEO_Study_2010.pdf

10. Deloitte, 2014. *The Deloitte Millennial Survey*. www.deloitte.com/millennialsurvey

11. Warnell, J. M. 2012. "Giving Voice to Values: Engaging Millennials and Managing Multigenerational Cultures," *Managing Human Resources from the Millennial Generation*. Charlotte, NC: Information Age, pp. 117–37.

12. Bias, S. K., and Phillips, D. L. 2012. "Implications of Values of the Millennial Generation on HR Infrastructure," *Managing Human Resources from the Millennial Generation*. Charlotte, NC: Information Age, pp. 301–21.

13. Stewart, K., and Bernhardt, P. 2010. "Comparing Millennials to Pre-1987 Students and with One Another," *North American Journal of Psychology 12*, no. 3, pp. 579–602.

14. Philips, M. "There Are More 23-Year-Olds than Any Other Age (and They're Going to Save the World)," *Time Magazine*, June 26, 2014.

15. Ibid.

16. Gentile, 2010.

17. Gentile, 2010, p. xxiii.

18. Warnell, 2012.

19. Rushworth, M. K. 2005. *Moral Courage: Taking Action When Your Values Are Put To the Test*. New York: William Morrow, HarperCollins.

20. Gentile, 2008.

21. Gentile, 2010.

22. Gentile, 2010.

23. Gentile, 2010.

24. McGlone, T., Spain, J., and McGlone, V. (2011). "Corporate Social Responsibility and the Millennials," *Journal of Education for Business 86*, no. 4, pp. 195–200.

25. Aspen Institute. 2008. "Where Will They Lead? MBA Student Attitudes about Business and Society," http://www.aspeninstitute.org/publications/where-will-they-lead-2008-executive-summary-pdf

26. Gentile, M. C. 2008. *Ways of Thinking about Our Values*. www.GivingVoiceToValues.org

27. Gentile, 2010.

28. George, B., and Baker, D. 2011. *True North Groups: A Powerful Path to Personal and Leadership Development*. San Francisco: Berrett-Koehler.

29. Myers, K. E., and Sadaghiani, K. 2010. "Millennials in the Workplace: A Communication Perspective on Millennials' Organizational Relationships and Performance," *Journal of Business and Psychology 25*, pp. 225–38.

30. Deery, P. 2012. "Texts, E-Mails and Google Searches: Training in a Multigenerational Workplace," *Managing Human Resources from the Millennial Generation*. Charlotte, NC: Information Age, pp. 229–47.

31. This material has been included with permission from the *Giving Voice to Values* curriculum collection www.GivingVoice and www.MaryGentile.com, developed by Mary C. Gentile. The Aspen Institute was founding

partner, along with the Yale School of Management, and incubator for Giving Voice to Values (GVV). Now Funded by Babson College.

32. Gentile, M. C. 2008. "Tale of Two Stories," www.GivingVoiceToValues.org

33. Gentile, 2008.

34. Gentile, 2010.

35. Bazerman, M. H., and Tenbrunsel, A. E. 2011. *Blind Spots: Why We Fail To Do What's Right And What To Do About It.* Princeton, NJ: Princeton University Press.

36. Carnegie Council for Ethics in International Affairs, Interview with Mary C. Gentile, https://www.carnegiecouncil.org/studio/multimedia/20120327/transcript.html?withOthers=1, accessed May 27, 2012.

37. During this exercise, you are reminded to honor any obligations of confidentiality that you may have with current or past employers.

38. In this exercise, a "values conflict" refers to a disagreement that has an ethical dimension to it. That is, I might disagree with your idea about the most efficient process flow design for an assembly line, but there is usually not an ethical component to that decision. However, if one design reflected a commitment to worker safety or environmental concerns and the other did not, for example, even this disagreement might be appropriate here.

39. McAfee, A. 2010. "How Millennials' Sharing Habits Can Benefit Organizations," *Harvard Business Review, 88.* http://blogs.hbr.org/hbr/mcafee/2010/08/how-millennials-sharing-habits.html

40. Ibid.

41. Keengwe, J., and Georgina, D. 2013. "Supporting Digital Natives to Learn Effectively with Technology Tools," *International Journal of Information and Communication Technology Education 9*, no. 1, pp. 51–9.

42. IGI Global. April 21, 2014. "Millennials Don't Stand A Chance," www.igi-global.com/newsroom/archive;/millennials-don-stand-chance/1840/

43. Holmes, R. August 23, 2012. "Social Media Compliance Isn't Fun, But It's Necessary," Harvard Business Review, *HBR Blog Network.* http://blogs.hbr.org/2012/08/social-media-compliance-isnt/

44. Ibid.

45. Ibid.

46. Ibid.

47. Ethics Resource Center. 2013. *National Business Ethics Survey of Social Networkers: New Risks and Opportunities at Work.* http://www.ethics.org/resource/national-business-ethics-survey%C2%AE-social-networkers-nbes-sn-risks-and-opportunities-work, p. 11.

48. DeGeorge, R. 1999. *Business Ethics.* 7th ed. New York, NY: Pearson.

49. Ethics Resource Center. 2013. *National Business Ethics Survey of Social Networkers.*

50. Ibid., p. 9.

51. Ethics Resource Center. 2013. *National Business Ethics Survey of Social Networkers.*

52. Ibid., p. 10.

53. Distasio, S., and Lord, D. 2014. "Is Social Networking Good for Learning?" *Chief Learning Offi*cer. http://www.clomedia.com/articles/5790-is-social-networking-good-for-learning?interstitial=RS090814

54. Ibid.

55. Ibid., p. 10.

56. Ibid., p. 11.

57. Keengwe, J., and Georgina, D. 2013. "Supporting Digital Natives to Learn Effectively with Technology Tools," *International Journal of Information and Communication Technology Education 9*, no. 1, pp. 51–9.

58. Gentile, M. C. *Guidelines for Peer Coaching.* www.GivingVoiceToValues.org

59. Association for Talent Development. 2014. *Playing to Win: Gamification and Serious Games in Organizational Learning.* http://www.astd.org/Publications/Research-Reports/2014/Playing-to-Win.

60. Pavia-Higel, L. 2014. "Using 'Mulligans' to Enhance Student Participation and Reduce Test Anxiety," *Faculty Focus.*

61. Leonardi, P., Neeley, T., and Gerber, E. 2012. "How Managers Use Multiple Media: Discrepant Events, Power, and Timing in Redundant Communication," *Organization Science 23*, no. 1.

62. Meister, J. C. and Willyerd, K. 2010. "Mentoring Millennials." *Harvard Business Review.* https://hbr.org/2010/05/mentoring-millennials

63. Krause, A., and Basile, G. 2014. "Can Millennials and Social Networking Lead Us to a Sustainable Future?" *GreenBiz.com.* http://www.greenbiz.com/blog/2014/05/20/can-millennials-and-social-networking-lead-us-sustainable-future?page=full

64. Ibid.

65. "Rival Corporate Giants Join Forces to Get Millennials Acting on Climate Change," *The Guardian.* http://www.theguardian.com/sustainable-business/2014/oct/06/-sp-millenials-business-coke-pepsi-nestle-climate-change-collectively, accessed October 6, 2014.

66. Krause and Basile. 2014.

67. Straumsheim, C. "Social Media May Benefit International Students and Group Projects, Researchers Argue," *Inside Higher Ed.* http://www.insidehighered.com/news/2014/04/07/social-media-may-benefit-international-students-and-group-projects-researchers-argue, accessed April 7, 2014.

68. Toosi, M. 2012. "Labor Force Projections to 2020," *Monthly Labor Review 135*, pp. 43–64.

69. Eisner, S. 2012. "Best Practices for Managing Generation Y," *Managing Human Resources from the Millennial Generation*. Charlotte, NC: Information Age, pp. 251–78.

70. Auriemma, A. "Zappos Zaps Its Job Postings: Online Shoe Retailer Creates Social-Media Network to Evaluate Potential Hires," *Wall Street Journal.* May 26, 2014.

71. Ibid.

72. Weinberg, C. July 18, 2014. "Keeping Millennials Happy Is Now Its Own Genre of Management Training," *Bloomberg Businessweek.*

73. Eisner, 2012.

74. Taylor, P. 2014. *The Next America: Boomers, Millennials and the Looming Generational Showdown.* New York, NY: Public Affairs, Perseus Books.

75. Ibid.

76. Deery, P. 2012. "Texts, E-Mails and Google Searches: Training in a Multi-generational Workplace," *Managing Human Resources from the Millennial Generation.* Charlotte, NC: Information Age. pp. 229–47.

77. Hampton, K., Rainie, L., Lu, W., Dwyer, M., Shin, I., and Purcell, K. 2014. *Social Media and the "Spiral of Silence."* http://www.pewinternet.org/2014/08/26/social-media-and-the-spiral-of-silence/

78. Goudreau, J. *14 Rules Of The New Workplace That Millennials Need To Master.* http://www.businessinsider.com/millennials-need-to-learn-these-14-rules-2013-9#ixzz34G4U5iF4

79. Hess, A. "Millennials Aren't Oversharing on Social Media," *Slate.com.* http://www.slate.com/blogs/xx_factor/2013/10/18/millennials_on_social_media_young_people_are_incredibly_savvy_about_internet.html

80. Ibid.

81. Snow, C., Miles, R., and Coleman, Jr., H. J. 1992. "Managing 21st Century Network Organizations," *Organizational Dynamics 20*, pp. 5–20.

82. Pearce, C. L., Wassenaar, C. L., and Manz, C. C. 2014. "Is Shared Leadership the Key to Responsible Leadership?" *The Academy of Management Perspectives 28*, no. 3, pp. 275–88.

83. Ibid.

84. Ibid.

85. Myers and Sadaghiani, 2010.

86. Gentile, 2008.

87. Gentile, 2008.

88. Gentile, 2008.

89. Myers and Sadaghiani, 2010, p. 229.

90. Gentile, 2008.

91. Gentile, 2008.

92. Philips, M. May 22, 2012. "Boomers and Millennials: Who's Got It Worse in the Workplace?" *Bloomberg Businessweek*. http://www.businessweek .com/articles/2012-05-22/boomers-and-millennials-whos-got-it-worse-in-the-workplace

93. Ibid.

94. White, M. 2011. *Rethinking Generation Gaps in the Workplace: Focus on Shared Values.* University of North Carolina Kenan-Flagler Business School, UNC Executive Development, http://www.kenan-flagler.unc .edu/executive-development/custom-programs/~/media/C8FC09AEF-03743BE91112418FEE286D0.ashx

95. Erickson, T. February 16, 2009. "The Four Biggest Reasons for Genearational Conflict in Teams," *Harvard Business Review*, HBR Blog Network. http://blogs.hbr.org/2009/02/the-four-biggest-reasons-for-i/

96. Ibid.

97. Ibid.

98. Ibid.

99. Howe, N., and Hadler, R. February 2012. "Why Generations Matter: Ten Findings from LifeCourse Research on the Workforce," http://www .lifecourse.com/assets/files/Why%20Generations%20Matter%20Life-Course%20Associates%20Feb%202012.pdf.

100. Ibid.

101. Ibid.

102. Author-Led Student Focus Group. 2014. Quotations throughout the book presented in callout boxes are derived from a focus group with 22 senior undergraduate business students, with anonymous attribution by permission, conducted February 2014.

103. Eisner, 2012.

104. Ibid.

105. Agan, T. "Embracing the Millennials' Mind-Set at Work," *New York Times*, November 9, 2013.

106. Ibid.

107. Kitroeff, N. August 19, 2014. "Life is Actually Getting Easier for Goldman Sachs Interns," *Bloomberg Businessweek*.

108. Agan, 2013.

109. Hershatter, A., and Epstein, M. 2010. "Millennials and the World of Work: An Organization and Management Perspective." *Journal of Business and Psychology* 25, PP. 211–223.

110. Ibid.

111. Millennial B. "Millennial Branding and American Express Release New Study on Gen Y Workplace Expectations." http://millennialbranding.com/2013/ 09/gen-workplace-expectations-study/

112. Deloitte, 2014. *The Deloitte Millennial Survey.*

113. Crosson, M., Mazutis, D., Seijts, G., and Gandz, J. 2013. "Developing Leadership Character in Business Programs," *Academy of Management Learning & Education 12*, no. 2. *http://amle.aom.org/content/early/2012/07/26/amle.2011.0024A.abstract.*

114. Kopelman, S. May 15, 2014. "Corporate Ethics Slide Because of Bad Negotiations," *BloombergBusinessweek.* http://www.businessweek.com/articles/2014-05-15/narrow-approaches-to-teaching-negotiation-have-resulted-in-a-generation-of-leaders-who-make-ethical-compromise

115. Ibid.

116. Zhong, C. B., Bohns, V. K., and Gino, F. 2010. "A Good Lamp Is the Best Police: Darkness Increases Self-interested Behavior and Dishonesty," *Psychological Science 21*, no. 3, pp. 311–4.

117. Lang, J. 2013. *Cheating Lessons: Learning from Academic Dishonesty.* Cambridge, MA: Harvard University Press.

118. Bias and Phillips. 2012.

119. Ibid.

120. Sims, R. R. 2012. "Building Bridges Between the Millennials and Other Generations", *Managing Human Resources from the Millennial Generation.* Charlotte, NC: Information Age, pp. 421–44.

121. Kiviat, B. and Gates, B. "Making Capitalism More Creative," *Time* Magazine. July 31, 2008.

122. Christakis, N., and Fowler, J. 2001. *Connected: The Surprising Power of Our Social Networks and How They Shape Our Lives—How Your Friends' Friends' Friends Affect Everything You Feel, Think, and Do.* New York, NY: Back Bay Books.

123. Ibid.

124. Patton, C. June 6, 2014. "Study: CSR Encourages Better Customer Service," http://www.hreonline.com/HRE/view/story.jhtml?id=534357176.

125. Glavas, A., and Kelley, K. April 2014. "The Effects of Perceived Corporate Social Responsibliity on Employee Attitudes," *Business Ethics Quarterly 24*, no. 2.

126. Immelt, J. 2009. "Driving Innovation and Economic Renewal in a Global Context," *Keynote Presentation, Net Impact Conference.* Ithaca, New York.

127. Patton, 2014. "Study: CSR Encourages Better Customer Service."

128. Yu, Kun, Du, Shuili, and Bhattacharya, C. B. 2014. "Everybody's Talking But is Anybody Listening? Stock Market Reactions to Corporate Social Responsibility Communications," Harvard Business School Working Paper.

129. Coleman, J., and George, B. December 30, 2011. "Five Resolutions for Aspiring Leaders," *Harvard Business Review,* Harvard Working Knowledge.

130. Greene, J. D. 2003. "From Neural 'Is' to Moral 'Ought': What are the Moral Implications of Neuroscientific Moral Psychology?" *Nature Reviews Neuroscience 4*, pp. 847–50.

131. Smith, C. 2011. *Lost in Transition: The Dark Side of Emerging Adulthood.* New York, NY: Oxford University Press.

132. Jones, D. A., Willness, C. R., and Madey, S. 2014. "Why Are Job Seekers Attracted by Corporate Social Performance? Experimental and Field Tests of Three Signal-Based Mechanisms," *Academy of Management Journal 57*, no 2, pp. 383–404.

133. Friedman, T. L. "How To Get a Job at Google," *New York Times*, February 22, 2014.

134. Ethics Resource Center. 2013. "Generational Differences in Workplace Ethics: A Supplemental Report of the 2011 National Business Ethics Survey," www.ethics.org/nbes

135. Ibid.

136. Ibid.

137. Ibid.

138. Murray, A. "What Are the Common Mistakes of New Managers?" *Wall Street Journal*. April 7, 2009.

139. Murray, 2009.

140. Ibid.

141. Ibid.

142. Papke, E. September 22, 2014. "How Leaders Kill Innovation: And 4 Keys to Overcoming Them," *American Management Association*. http://playbook. amanet.org/leaders-kill-innovation-4-keys-overcoming/

143. Ibid.

144. Howe, N., and Strauss, W. 2000. *Millennials Rising: The Next Great Generation*. New York, NY: Vintage Books, Random House.

145. Kaplan, R. S., and David, K. April 2004. "Accounting Fraud at World-Com," Harvard Business School Case 104-071 (Revised September 2007.)

146. Ethics Resource Center. 2013. "Generational Differences in Workplace Ethics."

147. Ethics Resource Center. 2013. "National Business Ethics Survey," www .ethics.org/nbes

148. Ibid.

149. Ibid.

150. Ruedy, N. E., Moore, C., Gino, F. and Schweitzer, M. E. 2013. "The Cheater's High: The Unexpected Affective Benefits of Unethical Behavior," *Journal of Personality and Social Psychology 105*, no. 4, pp. 531–48.

151. Ariely, D. 2013. *The Honest Truth about Dishonesty: How We Lie to Everyone—Especially Ourselves*. New York, NY: Harper Perennial.

152. Myers and Sadaghiani, 2010.

153. Beer, M., Eisenstat, R. A., Foote, N., Fredberg, T., and Norrgren, F. 2011. *Higher Ambition: How Great Leaders Create Economic and Social Value.* Boston, MA: Harvard Business Press.

154. Mackey, J., and Sisodia, R. 2013. *Conscious Capitalism: Liberating the Heroic Spirit of Business.* Boston, MA: Harvard Business Review Press.

155. George, B. June 5, 2014. "Fixing the 'I Hate Work' Blues," *Harvard Working Knowledge.* http://hbswk.hbs.edu/item/7547.html

156. Ibid.

157. Trevino, L., Hartman, L., and Brown, M. Summer 2000. "Moral Person and Moral Manager: How Executives Develop a Reputation for Ethical Leadership," *California Management Review 42,* no. 4. pp. 128–142.

158. Ibid.

159. Christensen, L. J., Mackey, A., and Whetten, D. 2014. "Taking Responsibility for Corporate Social Responsibility: The Role of Leaders in Creating, Implementing, Sustaining or Avoiding Socially Responsible Firm Behaviors," *The Academy of Management Perspectives 28,* no 2, pp. 164–78.

160. Myers and Sadaghiani, 2010.

161. Meister and Willyerd, 2010.

162. Ibid.

163. Ibid.

164. George, B., and Baker, D. 2011. *True North Groups: A Powerful Path to Personal and Leadership Development.* San Francisco: Berrett-Koehler.

165. Di Stefano, G., Gino, F., Pisano, G., and Staats, B. "Learning by Thinking: How Reflection Aids Performance," Harvard Business School NOM Unit Working Paper No. 14-093, March 25, 2014.

166. Nobel, C. "Reflecting on Work Improves Job Performance," *Harvard Business Press Working Knowledge,* May 5, 2014.

167. Di Stefano, Gino, Pisano, and Staats. 2014.

168. Brack, J. 2012. "Maximizing Millennials in the Workplace," University of North Carolina Kenan-Flagler Business School, UNC Executive Development, http://www.kenan-flagler.unc.edu/executive-development/custom-programs/~/media/DF1C11C056874DDA8097271A1ED48662.ashx

169. Nikravan, L. August 8, 2014. "Handing Over the Keys: From Baby Boomers to Millennials," *Chief Learning Officer.*

170. Groysberg, B., and Slind, M. June 2012. "Leadership is a Conversation," *Harvard Business Review.* https://hbr.org/2012/06/leadership-is-a-conversation.

171. Ibid.

172. Ibid.

173. Ibid.

174. Quatro, S. A. 2012. "Millennial-centric Strategic HR: Key Practices for Attracting, Developing, and Retaining Millennials," *Managing Human Resources from the Millennial Generation*. Charlotte, NC: Information Age, pp. 323–33.

175. Sims, R. R. 2012. "Building Bridges Between the Millennials and Other Generations", *Managing Human Resources from the Millennial Generation*. Charlotte, NC: Information Age, pp. 421–44.

176. Weinberg, 2014.

177. Pink, Daniel. 2009. *Drive: The Surprising Truth about What Motivates Us*. New York, NY: Penguin Group.

178. Ibid.

179. Ibid.

180. Ibid.

181. Ibid.

182. Ibid.

183. Deloitte, III. April 7, 2014. *Annual Deloitte Core Beliefs & Culture Survey* http://www.deloitte.com/view/en_US/us/press/Press-Releases/f2ca7e803a 725410VgnVCM1000003256f70aRCRD.htm

184. Govindarajan, V., and Srinivas, S. August 6, 2013. "The Innovation Mindset in Action: 3M Corporation," *Harvard Business Review Blog Network*. http://blogs.hbr.org/2013/08/the-innovation-mindset-in-acti-3/

185. Ibid.

186. Deloitte, 2014. *The Deloitte Millennial Survey*. www.deloitte.com/ millennialsurvey

187. Ibid.

188. Enderle, G. 2009. "A Rich Concept of Wealth Creation Beyond Profit Maximization and Adding Value." *Journal of Business Ethics* 84, pp. 281–295.

189. Deloitte, 2014.

190. Ibid.

191. Coleman, J., Gulati, D., and Segovia, W. O. 2012. *Passion & Purpose: Stories from the Best and Brightest Young Business Leaders* New York, NY: Harvard Business Review Press.

192. Gentile, 2010.

193. Kidder, 2005.

194. Meister and Willyerd, 2010.

195. Beer, M., Eisenstat, R. A., Foote, N., Fredberg, T., and Norrgren, F. 2011. *Higher Ambition: How Great Leaders Create Economic and Social Value*. Boston, MA: Harvard Business Press.

196. Ibid.

197. Ibid.

198. Mackey, J., and Sisodia, R. 2013. *Conscious Capitalism: Liberating the Heroic Spirit of Business.* Boston, MA: Harvard Business Review Press.

199. Quatro, S. A. 2012. "Millennial-centric Strategic HR: Key Practices for Attracting, Developing, and Retaining Millennials," *Managing Human Resources from the Millennial Generation.* Charlotte, NC: Information Age, pp. 323–33.

200. George, B. June 6, 2011. "Why Leaders Lose Their Way," *Harvard Business School Working Knowledge.* http://hbswk.hbs.edu/item/6741.html.

201. Ibid.

202. Barsh, J., and Lavoie, J. April. 2014. "Lead at Your Best," McKinsey & Company Insights & Publications. http://www.mckinsey.com/insights/leading_in_the_21st_century/lead_at_your_best

203. Hollensbe, E., Wookey, C., Hickey, L., and George, G. October 1, 2014. "Organizations with Purpose," *Academy of Management Journal 57*, no. 5. Pp. 1227–1234.

204. Keller Fay Group. May 2014. Prepared for the Aspen Institute Business and Society Program, "Unpacking Corporate Purpose: A Report on the Beliefs of Executives, Investors and Scholars," http://www.aspeninstitute .org/sites/default/files/content/upload/Unpacking_Corporate_Purpose_ May_2014_0.pdf.

205. Padró, M. May 28, 2014. "Unrealized Potential: Misconceptions about Corporate Purpose and New Opportunities for Business Education," *The Aspen Institute Business & Society Program.* http://papers.ssrn.com/sol3/papers.cfm?abstract_id=2443352.

206. Ibid.

207. Ibid.

208. Himsel, D. 2014. "Business Schools Aren't Producing Ethical Graduates," *Bloomberg Businessweek*, August 6, 2014.

209. Porter, M. E., and Kramer, M. R. January–February 2011. "Creating Shared Value: How to Reinvent Capitalism—and Unleash a Wave of Innovation and Growth," *Harvard Business Review.* https://hbr.org/2011/01/the-big-idea-creating-shared-value.

210. Ibid.

211. Feintzeig, R. September 3, 2014. "Employees' Children Give Company an Earful on Social Causes," *Wall Street Journal.*

212. Bain, K. 2004. *What the Best College Teachers Do.* Cambridge, MA: Harvard University Press.

213. Esfahani, S. E., and Aaker, J. L. "Millennial Searchers," *New York Times*, November 30, 2013.

214. Ibid.

215. De Datta, R. 2014. "Don't Waste Your 20s at Google or McKinsey," *LinkedIn blog post*, https://www.linkedin.com/today/post/article/20140727232741-15381-don-t-waste-your-20s-at-google-or-mckinsey, accessed July 27, 2014.

216. Griswold, A. 2014. "The Lost Weekends: How are Enforced Saturdays Off Working Out for Young Bankers?" *Slate.com*, http://www.slate.com/articles/business/moneybox/2014/07/goldman_sachs_protected_week ends_young_bankers_want_money_not_time.html?wpsrc=sh_all_mob_em_ru, accessed July 29, 2014.

217. Schawbel, D. 2013. "You're Probably Wrong About Millennials," Harvard Business Review, *Blog Network*, http://blogs.hbr.org/2013/09/youre-probably-wrong-about-mil/, accessed September 3, 2013.

218. Ibid.

219. Scheef, D., and Thielfoldt, D. 2014. "Preparing Millennials for Leadership Success," *SmartBlog on Leadership* http://smartblogs.com/leadership/2014/07/25/preparing-millennials-for-leadership-success-2/, accessed July 25, 2014.

220. Ibid.

221. Ibid.

222. Ibid.

223. Ibid.

224. Ibid.

225. Meister and Willyerd, 2010.

226. Ibid.

227. Sims, R., and Felton, E. 2006. "Designing and Delivering Business Ethics Teaching and Learning. *Journal of Business Ethics 63*, no. 3, pp. 297–312.

228. Net Impact. 2012. *Talent Report: What Workers Want.* www.netimpact.org/whatworkerswant, accessed May 2012.

229. Pink, 2009.

230. Meyer, M. February 26, 2013. "Message from a Millennial: Why We Are the Way We Are," http://www.amanet.org/training/articles/Message-from-a-Millennial-Why-We-Are-the-Way-We-Are.aspx.

231. Cates, K. 2014. "Not All Professional Women Want to Lean In," *Bloomberg Businessweek*, http://www.businessweek.com/articles/2014-05-15/not-all-professional-women-want-to-lean-in, accessed May 15, 2014

232. Ibid.

233. Feldman, D., and Yu, E. June 18, 2014. "Millennials and the Social Sector: What's Next?" *Stanford Social Innovation Review*. http://www.ssireview.org/blog/entry/millennials_and_the_social_sector_whats_next.

234. Ibid.

235. Gentile, 2010.

236. Ibid.

237. Kidder, 2005.

238. Sims, R., and Brinkmann, J. 2003. "Enron Ethics (or: Culture matters more than codes)," *Journal of Business Ethics*, 45, no. 3, pp. 243–56.

239. Jenkins, R., and John I. January 27, 2012. *Open Letter to the University of Notre Dame Community.* http://articles.wsbt.com/2012-01-27/abuse_30672641

240. Warnell, 2012; Gentile, 2010.

241. Gentile, 2010.

242. Warnell, 2012.

243. Svyantek, D. J., Cullen, K. L., and Svyantek, F. L. H. 2012. *Managing Human Resources from the Millennial Generation.* Charlotte, NC: Information Age, pp. 53–75.

244. West, J. P. 2012. *Managing Human Resources from the Millennial Generation.* Charlotte, NC: Information Age, pp. 201–28.

245. Eisner, S. 2012. *Managing Human Resources from the Millennial Generation.* Charlotte, NC: Information Age, pp. 251–78.

246. Darcy, K., and Hanley, G. "Ethics and Compliance Programs: Moving from 'Good Enough to 'Great,' Deloitte Risk and Compliance," *Wall Street Journal.* April 14, 2014. http://deloitte.wsj.com/riskandcompliance/2014/04/14/ethics-and-compliance-programs-moving-from-good-enough-to-great/.

247. Collins, D. 2009. *Essentials of Business Ethics: How to Create Organizations of High Integrity and Superior Performance.* Hoboken, NJ: Wiley & Sons.

248. Ibid.

249. Corporate Survey was conducted online and includes self-reported data which may include minor variations. Spring 2014.

250. Gentile, 2010.

251. Deal, J., Altman, D., and Rogelberg, S. 2010. "Millennials at Work: What We Know and What We Need To Do (if anything)," *Journal of Business and Psychology 25*, no. 2, pp. 191–9.

252. Meister and Willyerd, 2010.

253. Gentile, 2008.

254. Christiansen, C., Allworth, J., and Dillon, K. 2012. *How Will You Measure Your Life?* New York, NY: HarperCollins.

255. Agnew, J. May 2013. "Managing Millennials: Can Science Help?" *PM eZine.* http://aubreydaniels.com/pmezine/managing-millennials-can-science-help

256. Ibid.

257. McManus, W. J. 2011. "'Ask More' of Business Education: Giving Voice to Values for Emerging Leaders," *Journal of Business Ethics Education: Special Issue: Giving Voice to Values 8*, no. pp. 320–5.

258. Manwani, H. 2013. "Profit's Not Always the Point," *TED.com*, Filmed October 2013.

259. McManus, 2010.

260. Author interview, 2014, company name withheld by request.

261. Robert J. Rutland Institute for Ethics, Clemson University. "The National Survey of CEOs on Business Ethics," https://www.clemson.edu/ethics/events/old_events/ceo_survey_key_points_revised.pdf

262. Robert J. Rutland Institute for Ethics, Clemson University.

263. Baden, D. 2014. "Look on the Bright Side: A Comparison of Positive and Negative Role Models in Business Ethics Education," *Academy of Management Learning & Education 13*, no. 2. pp. 154–170

264. Gentile, 2008, p. 23.

265. Ibid., pp. 24–5.

266. Zhang, T., Gino, F., and Margolis, J. D. "Does 'Could' Lead to Good? Toward a Theory of Moral Insight." Harvard Business School Working Paper Number: 14-118, June 2014.

267. Ibid.

268. Brack, J. 2012. "Maximizing Millennials in the Workplace." University of North Carolina Kenan-Flagler Business School, UNC Executive Development, http://www.kenan-flagler.unc.edu/executive-development/custom-programs/~/media/DF1C11C056874DDA8097271A1ED48662.ashx

269. Ibid.

270. Lang, J. 2013. *Cheating Lessons: Learning from Academic Dishonesty.* Cambridge, MA: Harvard University Press.

271. Higgins, T., and Summers, N. June 18, 2014. "GM Recalls" How General Motors Silenced a Whistle-Blower," *Bloomberg Businessweek*.

272. McCabe, D. L., Linda, K. T., and Kenneth, D. B. 1999. "Academic Integrity in Honor Code and Non-Honor Code Environments: A Qualitative Investigation" *The Journal of Higher Education 70*, no. 2, pp. 211–34.

273. Lang, J. 2013. *Cheating Lessons: Learning from Academic Dishonesty.* Cambridge, MA: Harvard University Press.

274. Adams, S. "Dilbert," *comic strip*, July 18, 1997, http://dilbert.com/strips/comic/1997-07-18/

275. McCabe, Linda, and Kenneth, 1999.

276. Zhang, 2014.

277. Kaplan, J. May 11, 2014. "Hiring, Promotions and Other Personnel Measures for Ethical Organizations," *Conflict of Interest Blog*, http://conflictofinterestblog.com/2014/05/hiring-promotions-and-other-personnel-measures-for-ethical-organizations.html

278. Murphy, P. E. 2013. "Ethics and Integrity in Business: Importance for the Recruiting Process," *Notre Dame Deloitte Center for Ethical Leadership*, http://ethicalleadership.nd.edu/assets/110978/ethical_recruiting_practices_guide_2ed_.pdf

279. Coleman, J. "Six Components of a Great Corporate Culture," *Harvard Business Review blog*, http://blogs.hbr.org/2013/05/six-components-of-culture/, accessed May 6, 2013.

280. Buchanan, L. "Core Values of the Top Small Company Workplaces," *Inc. Magazine*, http://www.inc.com/winning-workplaces/magazine/201106/core-values-top-small-company-workplaces.html, accessed June 2011.

281. Pitesa, M. and Thau, S. 2013. "Compliant Sinners, Obstinate Saints: How Power and Self-Focus Determine the Effectiveness of Social Influences in Ethical Decision Making," *Academy of Management Journal 56*, no 3, pp. 635–58.

282. Ibid.

283. Beardsley, S., and Clabby, K. 2014. To appear in forthcoming article, "Giving Voice To Values: A Values-Driven Approach to Leadership Development," by Mary C. Gentile, *SAM Advanced Management Journal Special Issue on The UN Global Compact and the PRME Initiative: Principles for Responsible Business and Responsible Management Education.*

284. Ibid.

285. Ibid.

286. Ibid.

287. Ibid.

288. Brack, J. 2012. "Maximizing Millennials in the Workplace." University of North Carolina Kenan-Flagler Business School, UNC Executive Development, http://www.kenan-flagler.unc.edu/executive-development/custom-programs/~/media/DF1C11C056874DDA8097271A1ED48662.ashx

289. Knox, N., and Murphy, M. "Charity as a Recruiting Tool," *CFO Journal, Wall Street Journal.*September 2, 2014. http://blogs.wsj.com/cfo/2014/09/02/more-firms-use-charitable-programs-as-a-recruiting-tool/.

290. Battarbee, K., Fulton, S. J., and Gibbs, H. S. 2014, "Empathy on the Edge: Scaling and Sustaining a Human-Centered Approach in the Evolving Practice of Design." http://www.ideo.com/images/uploads/news/pdfs/Empathy_on_the_Edge.pdf

291. Ibid.

292. Mazzoni, M. "Employee Engagement: The 'Human Thread' Between Sustainability and Results," *Triple Pundit.* http://www.triplepundit.com/2014/06/employee-engagement-human-thread-sustainability-business-results/, accessed June 10, 2014.

293. "The Cost of a Bad Reputation—The Impacts of Corporate Reputation on Talent Acquisition." October 2014. *CR Magazine.* http://www.commitforum.com/index.php/the-cost-bad-reputation-the-impacts-corporate-reputation-talent-acquisition/

294. Mazzoni, 2014.

295. Ibid.

296. Ibid.

297. Ibid.

298. Pérez-Peña, R. "Starbucks to Provide Free College Education to Thousands of Workers," *New York Times*, June 15, 2014.

299. Ibid.

300. Ibid.

301. Net Impact, 2012. *Talent Report: What Workers Want*. www.netimpact.org/whatworkerswant

302. Fromm, J. "10 Things Millennial CEOs Will Reimagine in America," http://www.forbes.com/sites/onmarketing/2014/04/08/10-things-millennial-ceos-will-reimagine-in-america/, accessed April 8, 2014.

303. Blount, S. "Yes, the World Needs More MBAs. Here's Why," *Bloomberg Businessweek*, May 13, 2014, http://www.businessweek.com/articles/2014-05-13/yes-the-world-needs-more-mbas-dot-heres-why

304. During this exercise, you are reminded to honor any obligations of confidentiality that you may have with current or past employers.

305. For more information on "Peer Coaching and Feedback," see Part 4 of "Scripts and Skills" in the Giving Voice to Values curriculum.

306. Audi, R. 2008. *Business Ethics and Ethical Business*. New York, NY: Oxford University Press.

307. DesJardins, J. 2013. *An Introduction to Business Ethics*. New York, NY: McGraw-Hill.

Index

THE GIVING VOICE TO VALUES ON BUSINESS ETHICS AND CORPORATE SOCIALRESPONSIBILITY COLLECTION

Mary Gentile, Editor

The Giving Voice To Values initiative teamed up with Business Expert Press to produce a collection of books on Business Ethics and Corporate Social Responsibility that will bring a practical, solutions-oriented, skill-building approach to the salient questions of values-driven leadership. Giving Voice To Values (GVV: www.GivingVoiceToValues.org)—the curriculum, the pedagogy and the research upon which it is based—was designed to transform the foundational assumptions upon which the teaching of business ethics is based, and importantly, to equip future business leaders to not only know what is right, but how to make it happen.

Other Titles in This Collection

- *Ethical Leadership in Sport: What's Your ENDgame?* by Pippa Grange
- *The ART of Responsible Communication: Leading With Values Every Day* by David L. Remund

Forthcoming Titles in This Collection

- *Business Ethics and Finance Clarifying Our Vocation* by Anthony Asher
- *Social Media Ethics Made Easy* by Joseph W. Barnes
- *Business Ethics: A Moral Reasoning Framework* by Annabel Beerel
- *Ethical Selling: Developing Skills for Win Win Customer Interaction* by Alice Alessandri
- *Leadership Ethics: Moral Power for Business Leaders* by Lindsay Thompson

Announcing the Business Expert Press Digital Library

Concise e-books business students need for classroom and research

This book can also be purchased in an e-book collection by your library as

- a one-time purchase,
- that is owned forever,
- allows for simultaneous readers,
- has no restrictions on printing, and
- can be downloaded as PDFs from within the library community.

Our digital library collections are a great solution to beat the rising cost of textbooks. E-books can be loaded into their course management systems or onto student's e-book readers. The **Business Expert Press** digital libraries are very affordable, with no obligation to buy in future years. For more information, please visit **www.businessexpertpress.com/librarians.** To set up a trial in the United States, please contact sales@businessexpertpress.com

CPSIA information can be obtained at www.ICGtesting.com
Printed in the USA
BVOW08s0543200315

392495BV00004B/10/P